PENGUIN

END OF T..._

Neelesh Misra is a correspondent with the Associated Press working out of its South Asia bureau in New Delhi. As correspondent with AP and earlier with *India Abroad*, he has covered some of the biggest stories of the past few years, including India's nuclear tests, the Kargil war, the Gujarat earthquake and the killing of the royals in Nepal. He is the author of *173 Hours in Captivity*, an account of the 1999 hijacking of an Indian Airlines plane from Kathmandu to Kandahar. In addition to his work as a journalist, Neelesh Misra, who belongs to Lucknow, is a movie buff and has written lyrics for Hindi films and scripts for Hindi plays.

Also by the same author:

173 Hours in Captivity: The Hijacking of IC 814

NEELESH MISRA

End of the Line

The Story of the Killing of the Royals in Nepal

PENGUIN BOOKS

PENGUIN BOOKS
Published by the Penguin Group
Penguin Books India Pvt Ltd, 11 Community Centre, Panchsheel Park, New Delhi
110 017, India
Penguin Group (USA) Inc., 375 Hudson Street, New York, New York 10014, USA
Penguin Group (Canada), 10 Alcorn Avenue, Toronto, Ontario, Canada M4V 3B2 (a
division of Pearson Penguin Canada Inc.)
Penguin Books Ltd, 80 Strand, London WC2R 0RL, England
Penguin Ireland, 25 St Stephen's Green, Dublin 2, Ireland (a division of Penguin Books Ltd)
Penguin Group (Australia), 250 Camberwell Road, Camberwell, Victoria 3124, Australia
(a division of Pearson Australia Group Pty Ltd)
Penguin Group (NZ), cnr Airborne and Rosedale Road, Albany, Auckland 1310, New
Zealand (a division of Pearson New Zealand Ltd)
Penguin Group (South Africa) (Pty) Ltd, 24 Sturdee Avenue, Rosebank, Johannesburg
2196, South Africa

Penguin Books Ltd, Registered Offices: 80 Strand, London WC2R 0RL, England

First published by Penguin Books India 2001

Copyright © Neelesh Misra 2001

All rights reserved

10 9 8 7 3 5 4

Typeset in *Sabon Roman* by SÜRYA, New Delhi
Printed at Anubha Printers, Noida

This book is sold subject to the condition that it shall not, by way of trade or otherwise,
be lent, resold, hired out, or otherwise circulated without the publisher's prior written
consent in any form of binding or cover other than that in which it is published and
without a similar condition including this condition being imposed on the subsequent
purchaser and without limiting the rights under copyright reserved above, no part of this
publication may be reproduced, stored in or introduced into a retrieval system, or
transmitted in any form or by any means (electronic, mechanical, photocopying, recording
or otherwise), without the prior written permission of both the copyright owner and the
above-mentioned publisher of this book.

For Neelima

Once a fair and stately palace . . .
                          —*Edgar Allan Poe*

Contents

Acknowledgements

ROYAL AFFAIRS IN Nepal have always been kept behind a curtain of secrecy that is inspired by respect, awe and fear. No one talks. The only ones who love to talk about the royalty are Nepal's fringe tabloids, which often peddle gossip, innuendo and fiction: one of them even named me as the person who helped a former Indian ambassador topple Girija Prasad Koirala's government!

In such a scenario, this book could not have been written without the help of friends who helped me get access to the truth and helped me sift fact from fiction. The pity is that most of them—including the close friends of the then-crown prince, Miss Devyani Rana and royal relatives—cannot be named.

Thank you, all you Deep Throats.

I wish to thank Beth-Duff Brown my bureau chief at The Associated Press, and all my other colleagues in the New Delhi newsroom, for being patient when I disappeared from the under-staffed office to write a book.

My deep gratitude to Mr Mohan Bahadur Pandey, principal press secretary at the Narayanhiti Palace, for all his help. A more personal thank you to his colleague and my friend, Sarad Bista, who faced a volley of my tiny queries day and night with a smile.

Thank you to Binaj Gurubacharya, my AP colleague

in Kathmandu, for helping me at every step, for answering my late-night queries grumpily and for lending me half-a-computer—the CPU—to work in my hotel room. Oh, for the other half of the computer (the monitor) and the cheer that he sheepishly spreads, thanks to AP photographer Binod Joshi. Must find the guy who owned the keyboard.

Thank you, Moon.

To Mr Yogendra Sakya, the owner of the Ambassador Hotel and many others in Nepal, and his wife Mrs Bindu Sakya, for their perspective and help. Thanks also to the cheerful and good-natured staff at the hotel, who bore my whims and translated the king's Nepali poems.

Thanks to the eyewitnesses of the massacre—including Mr Maheshwar Kumar Singh and retired Gen. Rabi Shumshere Rana—for their interviews and time, to Dr Khagendra Bahadur Shrestha, the royal physician, for sharing his warm experiences of King Birendra's youth and later days, and to Mr Jaiparatap Rana at the King Mahendra Trust for sharing King Gyanendra's conservation efforts.

Thanks to Dr Bhekh Bahadur Thapa, the Nepalese ambassador in New Delhi, for his perspective. Thanks to Mr Padmaratna Tuladhar, Nepal's human rights activist, for his time and analysis.

Thanks to senior Panchayat-era Nepalese journalists, most of all Mr Ram Chandra Neupane, former chief editor of the *Gorkhapatra*, for his guidance and help.

Thanks to other friends who helped me in my research and interviews, whom I cannot name. (I hate this.)

And a big thank you to Krishan Chopra, senior editor at Penguin, for being patient with my haphazard ways. It was a pleasure working with you.

Chapter One

A Family Outing

PICKLES. MILK. SUNFLOWER OIL. Cottage cheese.

The shopping list was growing at Nayan Raj Pandey's house in the web of lanes called Dilli Bazaar. Servants worked away in the three-storey red brick building in the heart of Kathmandu. Grass was trimmed and hedges pruned in the large lawn outside the apartments. The narrow, winding staircase to Pandey's top floor home was washed and scrubbed and washed yet again. Inside his house, the glass panels were cleaned with detergent, the sofa cushions were dusted, and the large framed pictures hung across the house were polished. In the kitchen, Pandey's daughter-in-law supervised the preparation of snacks.

It was Jyeshtha 19, 2058 on the Nepalese calendar— Pandey's seventieth wedding anniversary. For the outside world, it was 1 June 2001.

Pandey, 82, bald, soft-spoken, and with an amazing memory, was a priest. This entitled him to respect, but there was another reason why he was so sought after: he and his ancestors had together served as royal priests to most of the kings of the Shah dynasty, that had ruled the kingdom for more than 230 years. Pandey had been married to the shy and frail Jeev Kumari in 1931, when he was only twelve years old, not uncommon then. It was not a very lavish ceremony, but the guest list was an impressive one and heading it was the monarch, King Tribhuvan.

Seventy years later, another king had agreed, happily, to grace a small party today at Pandey's residence: King Tribhuvan's grandson, King Birendra Bir Bikram Shah Dev.

Pandey had been King Birendra's royal priest for years. He was retired now, but was still described as the king's favourite priest. In April 1963, Pandey had performed for the king the yagyopaveet ceremony, an initiation rite in which a Hindu wears the sacred and pure thread, and many other rituals since. The king was said to consult him on many important personal matters. Pandey had also accompanied the king on many of his travels to pilgrim centres in India. Even after Pandey relinquished his official title of 'Rajguru' or royal priest, the king continued to address him by that name.

The Pandey family had been looking forward to the king's visit for days now. Several weeks ago, Pandey had sent a letter to the king, saying his family had organized the celebration, and he would be honoured if the monarch could come. He had said he was aware the king had heart ailments, but would be grateful if he accepted the invitation. The reply was prompt. 'Of course I will come,' he sent word. Hours after the king went away, there would be reason to leave the occasion etched on their memories.

The day was plodding along. Across the city in the Narayanhiti Palace, King Birendra was popping his pills. It was something the bespectacled, good-natured, hugely popular monarch hated doing, but he was a reluctant follower of his doctors' advice. The king had resisted any treatment for years. He avoided taking medicines for as long as he could. But he had been forced to remain on a strict diet since a heart attack in November 1998. He had controlled his appetite and restricted his palate, but he refused to give up one thing the doctors hated: his cigar. He had tried to reduce it, but he could never stop smoking. He could not control his cholesterol. And he refused to let health concerns come in the way of his passion for adventure and high-altitude trekking.

Taken together, these indulgences were a doctor's nightmare.

King Birendra often had his personal physicians on tenterhooks. At fifty-five, he was the longest surviving monarch in the Shah dynasty. This did not make the task of Brigadier-General Khagendra Bahadur Shrestha, the royal physician, any easier: King Birendra's family had a history of cardiac problems. His father, King Mahendra, grandfather King Tribhuvan, his uncles and other ancestors had all suffered heart attacks before they reached the age of fifty. The crisis came for King Mahendra when he was waiting for prey on a machan, from which he was hunting in the southern forests of the Chitwan area. His ECG examination was done on the tree.

Pandey was aware of King Birendra's heart problems. He had considered holding the wedding anniversary get-together on the ground floor so that the king would not have to climb three flights of stairs to his apartment. But the king had agreed to climb all the way up.

Even if it was not scheduled, it would not have been

totally unexpected if the king had decided to skip protocol and sprinted up the stairs to meet the priest. King Birendra was known to spring surprises on people.

He sprang the biggest surprises decades ago, in the 1960s, after his education at the St Joseph's College in Darjeeling and at Eton College. He was then an adventurous crown prince in his teens. Incognito and dressed in an army uniform, he used to trudge with Dr Shrestha, his doctor and companion of many journeys, up the mountain slopes, to remote villages, and to picturesque lakes and rivers where they sat silently for hours, trying to catch fish. They crossed furious rivers on rickety boats. They leaped into the water and swam and splashed through the currents. They went hunting. They went to villages and joined in festive dances. They had a hearty laugh when they were told how the villagers reacted when they came to know that the young army officer who had rested in their village was the crown prince!

As the disguised crown prince, Birendra had once walked into the tent of an Indian consular official camping in a remote area. The official explained to them for hours, using complex maps and charts, the work the Indians were doing in the region. Then he sheepishly said: 'I have been told that the crown prince can come here any day. I am going to show him all this material.' Birendra and his doctor had just smiled.

Armed with his education in India and England, King Birendra had come back to Nepal with a cosmopolitan view of life, and a passion for oil painting and horse riding. He was the first of Nepal's kings to receive formal education. He would treasure his five-year education at Eton (1959–64) all his life, and would send his sons, the Crown Prince Dipendra and the younger Prince Nirajan, to study there.

The king had been the perfect gentleman as he grew up in England, getting punished only once at a scouting camp where he was found guilty of flooding the camping area by either cutting the hose pipes or uncorking taps to cause the deluge. On all other days, he was, as an irreverent former classmate would say, 'a very, very nice bloke'. The future king was often addressed by his classmates by the nickname of 'Nipple', a distortion of his country's name. His cosmopolitan thinking was sharpened by his stints at Tokyo University and at Harvard.

Years passed. In February 1970, he made Aiswarya Rajya Lakshmi Devi Rana, the daughter of an army general and a might-have-been ruler of Nepal, his bride. Two years later, on 31 January 1972, King Mahendra passed away and Birendra, at twenty-six, became king. Before his coronation, he had already begun to drift, away from the friends of his youth as he prepared for the duties to come. His eldest son, Dipendra, was born in 1971.

The new king could no longer indulge in his biggest passions, like flying helicopters. Kingship reduced his adventures, but his love for surprises remained. The biggest surprise he sprang on his nation was when he gave it democracy in 1990, after widespread and violent demands and protests. Birendra had gracefully bowed to the pro-democracy campaign that had had furious slogans shouted against him as well. He would become one of the best and most loved constitutional monarchs in the world.

The next five years were a sad phase for the

monarchy, when people feared to publicly praise the king. But in 1995, an extraordinary event happened.

The local hotels' association organized a street festival to commemorate King Birendra's fiftieth birthday. Tens of thousands of people began to pour into the King's Way, the broad avenue that leads to the palace.

The cheering, dancing crowd swelled to more than 50,000 people who were crammed on the road a few hundred yards from the palace. They were going out of control. The police tried to beat them back, but failed. Suddenly, the huge gates of the palace started opening behind their backs. Eager to see the thousands who had gathered to wish him at a time when the royals were out of favour in Nepal, the king had decided to get a personal view of the events. He asked his entire family to get ready—and stepped out on the streets, in the midst of the boisterous crowd. It was the closest the people would get to him, as King Birendra made his way through the crowds, followed by his two sons, his younger brother Prince Gyanendra, and ladies of the family.

The king's closest aides sometimes tried to peep into his mind, guess how his varied experiences since childhood had shaped his thinking. The zigzags of the king's life seemed to have steeled the monarch for a high degree of stress tolerance.

King Birendra grew up virtually as a prisoner in the Narayanhiti Palace during the last phase of the century-old aristocratic rule of the Rana regime, when Birendra's grandfather King Tribhuvan was trying to break off the Rana yoke. Those were the days when the royal family members could not meet anyone, or go anywhere, without the permission of the Rana prime ministers. In

1950, the five-year-old Birendra fled with his father and grandfather to India, which helped the king throw off Rana rule.

For a young boy who understood little of the country's complex politics, the uncertainty would have been crippling, especially in the most dramatic moments. Birendra had watched spellbound as King Tribhuvan handed guns to each passenger in the Indian ambassador's car—even his secretary who had never handled a gun—as the royal family fled the palace to the safety of the Indian Embassy. The king had given brusque orders: 'If anyone sees any trouble, just shoot.'

Soon after this turbulent upsurge, Birendra was thrown from the conservative, fortified ambience of his youth to the relatively unbridled freedom of a missionary school in India. And the freedom just seemed to explode in his face at Eton.

'His education must have confused him, rather than trained him,' said a top official who had known King Birendra for decades.

The king then went to the United States—the best training ground of democracy—and then returned to become an unquestioned autocratic ruler. After thirty years, he gave up all of the power with one stroke.

The diverse influences had made the king progressive as well as deeply conservative, but his guiding force was clear: his love for his people.

King Birendra offered, very rarely, public glimpses of being a caring husband and a caring human being.

A few years ago, the king travelled to Nagarkot, a mountain town a short drive away from the capital Kathmandu, where his brother-in-law Kumar Khadga Bir Bikram Shah had requested him to inaugurate his hilltop tourist resort. The king munched on a lavish lunch, chatted with tourism industry executives and admired the scenic beauty of the place. Then he started inquiring about the facilities that the resort provided for the welfare of the locally hired staff, mostly from nearby villages. The royal family and guests were flummoxed as King Birendra walked up to the quarters of one of the lower-rank staff and peeped into the bathroom, trying to see their living conditions.

In public appearances, the king and queen had started to seem informal and at ease, after years of stiff and rare appearances. The Nepalese people were becoming accustomed to not getting shocked if they saw the king and queen having a quiet lunch at a table across them in a restaurant near the Narayanhiti Palace.

It was a huge change in image from the days when the first public smile of the stern-faced Queen Aiswarya had made waves. In recent years, the king and queen seemed ageing gracefully, like elderly parents, especially after the magnificent wedding ceremony in 1997 of Princess Shruti, who was their only daughter.

The king could not do without often seeing Princess Shruti even after her marriage. She was the quintessential papa's girl.

Shruti, twenty-four, had studied at the Kanti Ishwori School in Kathmandu, also the primary school where both her brothers spent their early childhood. She took part in most school events, including drama and dance, and Shruti grew up with diverse interests, including painting, sports and martial arts. When her brothers were at the boys-only Budhanilkantha School, Shruti went to the St Mary's Convent, and then travelled to India to study in the Mayo College in Ajmer. At Mayo, where she stayed for two years, it was a completely new world for the soft-spoken young princess. She had so far spent a cloistered, protected childhood in her country where her every step was closely watched. Shruti's teachers would remember her years later as an excellent swimmer and an outstanding athlete. She was also unwittingly thrown into the limelight when her photographs with an Indian movie star were splashed in film magazines. Many in Nepal criticized her for 'lack of royal etiquette'. But contrary to the media image of a flamboyant, uncaring girl from a high-profile family, Shruti was known as obedient, patient, quiet and disciplined. She loved horse riding and was known as one of the best riders at Mayo College. She would love horses all her life, scraping out time to ride even when recuperating between two pregnancies.

Shruti would also be remembered as an unassuming student who sometimes loved shedding her royal baggage. A strike by all the staff members, except teachers, once crippled Mayo. Students had to work themselves, and Shruti was seen scrubbing and washing the dormitory. Although not known for her cooking, given the phalanx of chefs back home, Shruti was in the kitchen as well, lending a hand to her classmates as they cooked for the school. A frequent visitor to Ajmer during Shruti's stay was her elder brother, Dipendra, with whom she also travelled round Rajasthan.

When she returned home, Shruti took to painting, like her father who had also published a book of his oil paintings. Shruti specialized in oil and watercolour paintings, as well as charcoal and pencil drawings. In 1996, Shruti held her first solo exhibition. A month before she died, she agreed to be painted by Dutch artist

Ed Van der Kooij, who displayed his paintings in an exhibition.

She had another side to her as well. She had trained with experienced judokas for ten years, and in May 1999, her teachers Om Bahadur Thapa and Maha Lakshmi Shrestha, watched with pride at a mat in the country's police training academy, when the princess was awarded her black belt by former Japanese prime minister Ryutaro Hashimoto.

People walking on the busy road in the crowded Thamel area, close to the palace, were pleasantly surprised one day when they saw a familiar couple walking down the road. They were walking to their daughter's home for a cup of tea, unannounced and without any bodyguards surrounding them. For King Birendra, there were now two other young ladies whose attention he frequently sought: Shruti's two daughters.

King Birendra had also nurtured his love for the mountains all his life. He was looking to yet another of those visits in the coming week: a journey to the spectacular Rara Lake at 10,000 feet, in Nepal's far west, surrounded by lofty hill slopes draped in pine and rhododendron. The king was going much higher than 8,000 feet, the height beyond which he was strictly advised against travelling. His cardiologists weren't happy.

As the sunny Friday wore on, the king worked in his office. Officials in the royal secretariats were busy planning his upcoming visits. The king's chief aide-de-camp, Sundar Pratap Rana, was tying up the logistics for the visit to the western region. Across the palace premises, in another office, the press secretariat was engaged in more elaborate planning. In July, the king was scheduled to undertake a state visit to Morocco, from where he would fly to London for his medical examination. This time, the king wanted to get the British doctors' stamp on his high-altitude ambitions, so that the frowns of his royal doctors would not deter him.

The press secretary had requested the king to instruct them about his preference for dates for travelling to Morocco and Britain.

'I will let you know on Monday,' he said. Dr Shrestha's concerns about the king's health had been on high alert after a November evening in 1998, when the telephone rang at his residence. It was Queen Aiswarya Rajya Lakshmi Devi Shah herself on the line, speaking nervously from the winter residence of the king, the Nagarjun Palace.

'His Majesty is having chest pain and indigestion. Please come quickly. Bring the ECG machine also,' the queen said.

It was the moment Dr Shrestha had dreaded for years. He alerted the military hospital—the designated hospital for royals, according to protocol, and rushed to the palace. The king was in pain. A quick ECG test showed the fears were true: King Birendra had suffered an acute heart attack.

That was just Problem One.

Problem Two: The king refused to be taken to a hospital.

Problem Three: The stern queen refused to let any other experts come and examine the king in the Nagarjun Palace.

Dr Shrestha continued treating the king with a cardiologist for days, and the queen allowed five other cardiologists to give their opinion on the monarch's health only in the Narayanhiti Palace. A cardiologist was instead flown in from Britain, where the king travelled two weeks later for a thorough medical check-up.

On 1 June, another medical check-up was being readied for a young boy.

Hom Bahadur, sixteen, is an orphan. Hom was a baby when his parents abandoned him at the Bal Mandir orphanage. It seemed the only way out to his sick and poverty-stricken father to try and ensure a respectable future for his son. On the next day, Queen Aiswarya came visiting as part of her numerous social service initiatives. She walked around the orphanage and met several children. As she was about to leave, Hom started wailing and clutched the queen's sari. The queen was overcome and picked him up. Hom was soon in the palace—the queen said she would take care of him.

He stayed in the palace for more than three years. The queen's younger son, Prince Nirajan, and her daughter, Princess Shruti, treated him with love—and the queen often fed him herself. Crown Prince Dipendra was away at Eton. Hom returned to the orphanage after some years, and started studying at the Kanti Ishwori Shishu Vidyalaya but the queen kept track of him. In the last few years, Hom had started suffering from very poor eyesight that threatened his continuation in school, and on Thursday, he had been admitted on the queen's instructions to the Tilganga Hospital for an operation. This was due on Friday.

The intense compassion for Hom Bahadur was one aspect of Queen Aiswarya's personality that had endeared her to the orphan boy. She was a creative person—in 1986, she had written a collection of lyrical poems under the pen name of Chandani Shah, and the lyrics were good enough to be set to music and to be translated into English, Hindi, Urdu, Bengali and Sanskrit. She was formally trained in music and loved gardening. She passionately loved flowers and had often asked some tourism industry executives to explore the possibility of growing tulips in Nepal.

But the queen's attention to Hom Bahadur hurt her eldest son, who had desperately tried for years to gain her attention and love, and failed. Dipendra was hurt that the queen often humiliated her eldest son, but was so loving towards the orphan.

But there were facets of the fifty-two-year-old queen's personality that could sometimes elicit strong reactions. Ever since her marriage to King Birendra, the queen had rapidly asserted herself in the royal affairs and was believed to have a powerful influence on the king's decisions.

Dipendra's thirtieth birthday was approaching, and he would often remember his humiliation on his last birthday. A celebration was taking place at the palace, when the birthday boy was ready to cut the cake. He walked over to Queen Aiswarya and said: 'Mua (mother), please come, it's time to cut the cake.'

The queen's reply, in front of the entire family, was short and snappy: 'Well, if you are grown up to do everything else on your own, why do you now need me to come to cut the cake?' She did not touch the birthday cake.

The queen decided the direction that her eldest son's life would take, the responsibilities he would be given, the prominence he would have in public life, and a key issue in Dipendra's life: the woman he would be allowed to marry.

The beautiful woman Dipendra wanted to marry was across town right now, working out at a gym. Today was a rare day—Devyani Rana and the crown prince had not been able to meet. But by late evening, they would have spoken on the phone at least eight times. Dipendra and Devyani had been passionately in love for more than two years now, and had known each other for much longer. Rana was the daughter of Pashupati Shumshere Rana, an influential political leader in Nepal, and Usha Rana, a member of the royal family of Gwalior in central India. The queen—partly because of her overbearing, insecure streak, and partly because she thought the Rana clan was lower in status—strongly disapproved of the match.

On their part, Devyani's family dreaded to think of their daughter getting married into a home where Queen Aiswarya made all the decisions and everything was done her way. It was an uncomfortable prospect for a girl's concerned parents.

Lately, there had been another cause of serious concern and fear. Devyani Rana had begun to perceive that her life was in danger. According to her closest relatives, she had started getting threatening calls, asking her to quit the relationship. The identity of the callers remained unknown.

For Dipendra, all this was adding up.

Queen Aiswarya had, in fact, disapproved of most decisions her eldest son had taken for a long time. Frustration and anger had been building up and Dipendra had come to strongly dislike his mother. He believed that she had a streak of vengeance towards him, and was much harder on him than on her other two children.

Some of that frustration was creeping up again. It was past 2:30 p.m. The royal family had had lunch in the large dining room.

They were scheduled to finish their engagements for the day and assemble at 7:30 p.m. in another part of the palace, in the Billiard Room close to Dipendra's residence. It was a routine party, held on the third Friday of each month, according to the Nepali calendar. Close family members and some other relatives were invited. The guest list was kept small, and the gathering exclusive: before the lunch, palace officials had called some of Dipendra's cousins, who had been invited, to politely request them not to come.

Soon after, the crown prince took off from the Tribhuvan Sadan, where his royal quarters were located, in his grey Land Cruiser. His ADCs accompanied him.

Dipendra did not have a good reputation around town as a driver, but today he seemed a little too merciless on the accelerator. The vehicle whizzed through the streets, veering between traffic, avoiding other cars and pedestrians. The crown prince was restless. He had to drive towards Jawalakhel. According to eyewitnesses, halfway through, he took a sudden turn from the Koteshwar intersection, driving left instead of right, screeched and started driving towards the ancient city of Bhaktapur. Stunned residents of the area had rarely watched him drive so recklessly. Some time later, he drove back towards his original destination.

Dipendra was scheduled to be on a tour of different sports complexes in the city. For him, today was the beginning of a very busy stretch of almost two weeks.

Nepal's biggest sporting event—the week-long Fifth National Games—was scheduled to be inaugurated on Sunday, 3 June, by the king at the Birendra International Sports Complex. Dipendra, who had a keen interest in sports, was the patron of the National Sports Council and the Nepal Olympic Committee. He would be the chief organizer of the national games. The massive event would draw teams from across the country, many of which had already started arriving in the capital. Planning had started months in advance, and there would be contests in a series of events, including swimming, soccer, shooting, squash, table tennis and lawn tennis.

He first went to the table tennis complex near the British Embassy, then drove to the stadium to inspect the other facilities. Dipendra had earned his name as a good sports administrator since he spearheaded the coordination of the South Asian Federation Games in 1999.

His interest in sports matched that of King Birendra. The king had started the national games, three of which had been held in different cities. King Birendra loved soccer, and his strong patronage to the sport was credited for Nepal's silver medal-winning performance at the Bangkok Asian Games.

For a few years now, Dipendra himself was providing Nepalese sports the punch it needed. He was a good sportsman himself, a master of martial arts and boxing.

Dipendra parked his car by the swimming complex and walked to the poolside, flanked by his guards. Top players splashed around, practising for the big contests. The crown prince had a keen eye and the officials of the swimming association had answers ready for most of his queries.

Satisfied, Dipendra walked to his favourite part of the sports facility—the shooting complex. Backed by Dipendra's patronage and efforts, the complex had been built to international standards. There were different ranges—50 metres, 25 metres and 10 metres—where shooters were practising. As he walked around, he occasionally stopped to speak to team members, many of whom were part of the national squad and familiar to him. The country's top players were there, including the men's champion, Asim Yadav, and the women's shooting champion, Bhagwati K.C.

Dipendra walked up to them.

'Is everything OK? All set for the competition?' he asked cheerfully.

After approximately twenty minutes, he walked out of the complex and drove to the brand new squash court, a few hundred metres away. A caravan of officials and government ministers followed in different cars.

Dipendra was seeing this court for the first time. He walked into the court, bent low to feel the wooden surface, then waited for several minutes until two players could begin a game. He watched silently for a long time. Then it was time to go back. There was another engagement coming up: he had to accompany his parents to the residence of Nayan Raj Pandey, the former royal priest.

He turned to talk to the sports officials.

'Make sure everything is OK. Can you people pull through?' he asked. The officials nodded.

'My father will come tomorrow morning at 10:30 for an inspection. I will come at 10. I want all of you here at 9:30,' he told the officials.

Dipendra drove back to the palace and rested for

some time. At about 6:30 p.m., he started getting ready for the visit to the priest's residence. Prince Nirajan, the darling of the family, would not be able to accompany them.

Nirajan was tired and sleepy. He had written the last of his examinations hours ago for a Bachelor of Commerce degree at the local university. The lanky twenty-three-year-old prince wanted to spend time that night with his friends at a party they had hosted. But his father had insisted that he attend the evening party, where Queen Mother Ratna Rajya Lakshmi Devi Shah, other aunts and uncles and cousins would be present. Nirajan reluctantly agreed.

Nirajan was also an alumnus of Eton, like his father and elder brother. All the boys in the royal family had, in fact, had identical early education: first at the Kanti Ishwori Shishu Vidyalaya, a primary school, then at the British-government-run Budhanilkantha Boarding Secondary School until the 10th grade. He had gone to Eton in 1995 as a prince but had tried to enjoy life like any other student—he was rumoured to have started drug abuse, and disappeared from the campus for several days for merrymaking. When his parents got word, Queen Aiswarya and Crown Prince Dipendra rushed to London, found Nirajan and took him back to the school, managing to persuade the school authorities not to suspend him. Nirajan was being groomed in his elder brother's shadow in the ways of the royalty—he had even made a state visit to China in August 1996.

Nirajan was becoming a great admirer of his uncle, Prince Gyanendra, for the work he was doing in the field of conservation and wildlife. He had done research on possibly starting a campaign to protect endangered freshwater Gangetic dolphins, which are disappearing from the Karnali and Narayani rivers and the Royal Bardiya National Park.

Nirajan was better at sports than his elder brother. He was a junior swimming champion at the Budhanilkantha School. He also loved horse riding, and his instructors saw in him the perfect attributes for a great future in the sport. 'His alertness and physique were perfect for riding . . . if he had tried, he could have made real achievements,' his former instructor Shishir Chandra Shah would say later. In recent years, he had developed a keen interest in soccer. Like his elder brother, Nirajan was closer to his father than to the queen.

Leaving Nirajan resting at the palace, King Birendra, the queen and the crown prince left the palace for Pandey's residence. Sirens blared and people paused to look as the royal motorcade, with the king and queen in a bullet-proof black Mercedes, wove through narrow roads and roundabouts towards Dilli Bazaar. The motorcade drove up a sharp slope and turned into the narrow lane, coming to a halt outside the three-storey building where dozens of people had been waiting. They were dressed in their best, and huge smiles broke on their faces as they arrived.

As he stepped out of the car, the king was in great spirits. The queen was somewhat stolid, but responsive. The crown prince was cold. If Dipendra was restless at the stadium, his mood had turned sour by the time he reached the priest's residence. There was something that had been playing on his mind for hours, and as the evening progressed, it seemed to tighten its grip.

The three royal guests stood in front of the cars as

Pandey performed a welcome ceremony. Hundreds of people were watching from nearby rooftops and street corners. Pandey stood before the king, queen and the crown prince, holding silver coins in his palm, and threw them on the ground before them, one by one, as a humble offering to the king. The royal chauffeur promptly picked up the coins and slipped them into his pocket.

The Pandey family worshipped King Birendra—revered as an incarnation of the Lord Vishnu in the kingdom—with a silver tray decorated with several oil wick lamps.

A red carpet had been laid on the pebbled ground. Dozens of people lined up along the carpet and threw fistfuls of rice flakes and flowers on the royal guests in welcome. The king smiled as the flakes fell on him. Then the royal family disappeared into the building. King Birendra climbed up the brown marbled stairs, a shadow of his energetic, adventurous teenage self.

They walked into the priest's home, plastered with framed pictures of the king himself and his forefathers. The king and queen settled comfortably on a sofa with brown floral patterns. Fat, comfortable satin pillows used by aristocrats, embroidered in gold, were placed behind both. Tea was served on a table before them.

No one would be allowed to sit on that sofa again. It would be adorned by large pictures of the king and queen.

Some metres away, the sullen crown prince sat beneath a huge mirror with an ornate frame. He spoke barely a few words.

The priest's family appeared from inside rooms in a well-rehearsed parade: each member folded hands in namaste and disappeared again inside the rooms. Then a little infant was brought in. This was the great-grandson of the priest, who had, earlier that day, tasted his first grain in a lavish ceremony called annaprashan. The priest carried out another round of offerings, this time placing two gold coins on silver plate. The king touched them and they were carried away. He could not accept an offering from his guru.

It was a room full of pictures. On one side, Pandey's ancestors, all royal priests, peeped out of yellowing photographs in small wooden frames. On the same wall was a huge photograph of the king and queen in their palace, with their signatures. Across the room, Queen Aiswarya's portrait on a china platter stood out in a collection of small mementos.

Hazy evening light filtered in through pink window curtains fluttering in the breeze.

'Your Majesty, your subject wishes to recite a Sanskrit hymn in your honour,' Pandey said with folded hands. The king smiled and gave his assent. The room fell silent. The priest cleared his throat. 'I will sing a religious poem. Kindly listen carefully, all,' Pandey said as he started reciting.

Thou owner of jewel-studded palaces and
    unfathomable riches,
Lord, what shall I offer you?
Thou master of the stunningly beautiful goddess-
    like Lakshmi,
Lord, what shall I offer you?
I could offer all at your feet if you were someone
    who was in need—
Lord, what shall I offer you?
Only one thing is lacking in you, My Lord—

You have given away your heart to a beautiful
        maiden . . .'

The king looked up at the priest, puzzled. People in his
position were not made the subject of romantic-sounding
poetry. Pandey hastily completed his poem.

You have given away your heart to a beautiful
        maiden . . .
And that is what I offer you my Lord—my
        mind, my soul, my heart.

The king broke into a smile. Pandey had won him over
yet again.

Then snacks were served. The king had some leavened
bread made of moong pulses, avoiding the other delicious
preparations: a cottage cheese cooked with vegetable in
thick gravy, pickles, pancakes, kheer, or sweetened rice
cooked in thick milk, and several other dishes.

'I am under strict dietary restrictions, guru,' the king
told Pandey.

'They are all cooked in sunflower oil, keeping your
health in mind, Your Majesty,' Pandey said. The queen
was enjoying every dish. She leaned over to her left and
whispered loudly in the king's ear: 'The kheer is very
nice.'

The crown prince refused to have anything, ignoring
Pandey's repeated requests.

'At least have Coke, your Royal Highness,' the
priest said. Dipendra refused. He mostly looked around
emotionless or stared at a golden coloured clock on the
facing wall.

The king had spent more than an hour chatting with
the priest. Finally, it was time to leave.

As he got up to go, the king spotted the priest's prayer room, facing the drawing room. He stood outside and folded his hands. His queen walked inside, sitting cross-legged on the floor as she offered a prayer to the array of deities.

The whole family then walked the royal guests down the stairs. As the king was about to step into his car, he turned back.

'Thank you,' he said to the priest and drove away.

Chapter Two

An Embattled Nation

OUTSIDE THE NARAYANHITI Palace, across the remote mountainous towns and villages, King Birendra's country of 24 million—one of the ten poorest in the world—was in disarray.

He could blame two men for that.

One of them lived in a two-storey red brick building, next door to Keshav Prasad Upadhaya, the chief justice of the Supreme Court. He was the country's prime minister, the lanky and bespectacled Girija Prasad Koirala. The address of the other, a soft-spoken, sombre man around forty-seven years, was unknown. He lived somewhere in the country's midwest in his mountainous base, commanded an army of poorly equipped but fiercely passionate fighters, and wanted to wipe out the monarchy. He was 'Prachanda', or The Fierce One, a man whose real name was Pushpa Kamal Dahal, the supreme leader of Nepal's powerful Maoist revolution.

Discontent swept through the capital. The Maoist revolution swept through the hinterland. Both were provoked by poor governance, power-hungry politicians, massive unemployment, allegations of government corruption and soaring levels of poverty. The government's popularity had plummeted since the last elections to the House of Representatives in May 1999, prompting large-scale street protests, and there seemed no hope of political stability: the country had had ten prime ministers in ten years. At least half the population earned wages below the minimum levels of sustenance. To many analysts, Nepal was a nation that was propping itself largely on foreign aid, grants and development projects.

This was not the nation that King Birendra had envisioned when he took over on 31 January 1972, or when he let go of absolute power on 9 November 1990 after the protests. The nation, often described as having one foot in the sixteenth century and the other in the twenty-first, was hobbling. It had been thrown badly off balance.

King Birendra had inherited an extremely underdeveloped nation. To a Westerner, the Nepal of those days would have seemed a massive jigsaw of villages. There were few roads. Travelling from one town to another often meant meandering all the way into India and back into Nepalese territory before reaching the destination. Development indices were extremely low—85 per cent of the citizens were illiterate, there were few doctors, and infant mortality was high: 172 children in 1,000 live births did not survive. When King Birendra's reign ended, a substantial part of the country remained without roads but the network had still increased fourfold. It included the 1,000-kilometre highway named after his father, running across the country.

Health programmes were showing success—the infant mortality rate was down to 80 per 1,000 live births.

The literacy rate had increased to 50 per cent. King Birendra had also set up institutions to make the country's media and judiciary more open and effective.

Even with an area of only 147,200 square kilometres, it was not an easy nation to govern. The pinnacle of its geographical diversity are seven of the world's highest peaks, including Mount Everest, the roof of the Earth, also known as Sagarmatha in Nepal. But across the land-locked country, the terai plains are located barely 300 metres above sea level, on the northern reaches of the fertile alluvial plains of the Ganga River. Irrigated land was only 8,500 square kilometres.

Apart from the geography, the people themselves form a rainbow culture. In the world's only Hindu state, members of this community form 90 per cent of the people, divided into numerous castes and sects. Buddhists form 5 per cent of the population and Muslims 3 per cent. More than twenty languages are spoken, split up into dozens of dialects.

Even though Nepal is an agriculture-dominant country where 80 per cent people survive off farming, there are no permanent crops. The people are also haunted by floods, landslides, thunderstorms, drought and even famine. The country is divided into three broad areas, the Mountain Region, the Hill Region, and the Terai Region, running in massive topographical belts across the country. Any administration had the massive task of adapting governance to this formidable geography.

The king tried to keep pace with the development projects, travelling to far-flung areas in the country in the icy winters to meet ordinary people. But the report card of King Birendra would still show him scoring much better grades as king than as administrator. Despite his good intentions, his tenure saw large-scale misrule. Nepal was still in the notorious thirty-year Panchayat Era.

The Panchayat Era took root in 1960 after King Mahendra sacked and arrested the first elected prime minister, B.P. Koirala, who had come to power a year ago. The veteran leader spent eight years in prison, and eight more in exile in India. Soon, behind his back, there would be an iron grip on the nation by the royal family and its nominees. King Mahendra appointed his own council of ministers in 1961, and outlawed political parties. An armed insurrection by the Nepali Congress in areas bordering India was swiftly crushed.

The Panchayat System was very democratic at face value: elections in 4,000 village councils set off a string of hierarchical elections that finally resulted in the selection of ninety members to the Panchayat, the then national assembly.

But in an era of partyless democracy, it was an assembly of toothless lawmakers.

The members could not bring, or vote on, or enact, bills without King Mahendra's approval. They could not criticize the king's government. They could not discuss the shortcomings of partyless democracy. The king appointed all high officials of the land, including the chief justice and top civil servants; he was the supreme commander of the armed forces, and he could veto any decision of the Supreme Court or the National Assembly, or amend the Constitution, as he liked. Nepal's king was god again, in myth and in reality.

But not so far away in history, the monarchy would pay the price.

Some turmoil began right away, with the enthronement of King Birendra. Approximately 100 armed attackers, allegedly linked to the exiled Koirala, attacked a village in the southern plains and killed a policeman. University students in Kathmandu went on a long and headline-catching strike. A year later, unidentified terrorists hijacked a Royal Nepal Airlines plane to India. In 1974, other armed attacks on the establishment continued.

The first milestone for the pro-democracy movement was the widespread unrest among students in 1979, which forced King Birendra to hold a referendum and introduce direct elections to the Rashtriya Panchayat. It was also a historic first step by him to break free from the autocratic spell of his father's era. King Birendra had become the first monarch in the history of Nepal to go to his subjects for their opinion. Approximately 4.8 million voters, of the 7.2 million eligible to vote, took part in the referendum on 2 May 1980.

It was a close call. Less than 55 per cent supported the Panchayat system. More than 45 per cent wanted it scrapped. After long years of governance without accountability, King Birendra introduced the first wave of reform. He paved the way for a prime minister answerable to the house. But the rumblings continued.

Before the big bang of public opinion, another catastrophe took place, this time carried out by neighbour India, which announced on 23 March 1989 that all trade and transit treaties with Nepal had expired. Except two, all the border entry points into Nepal from India—crucial for the supply of most goods—were closed. Nepal was thrown into chaos.

A year later, however, the anger of the Nepalese

people had shifted back to the palace, instead of India. The democracy campaign had exploded again, casting dark clouds over the Narayanhiti Palace during the upheaval of 1990.

For the first time in decades, the hero of the moment was not the king in the palace. It was a gutsy, sixty-six-year-old bachelor on the streets—Krishna Prasad Bhattarai, Nepali Congress leader and the anchor of the movement against the Panchayat Rule.

Bhattarai had honed his skills in India, where he had studied in Varanasi. During the British colonial era in 1945, he became the vice president of the Nepal Students Association, and founded a group called the Nepali Rashtriya Congress in 1947, when India threw off British rule and became independent. On 9 April 1950, the Nepali Congress, the main party that would lead the nation to democracy, was founded. Bhattarai had played with fire before he became a liberal political leader—in November 1951, he was one of the commanders of the armed activists who captured two districts in an attempted armed insurrection.

Bhattarai was the Speaker of the first elected Parliament in 1959, but was arrested and jailed for fourteen years in the clampdown by King Mahendra. He was granted amnesty in 1975, and was soon back at the forefront of the pro-democracy movement.

This time, Nepal's monarchy seemed at a point of no return. Its very future was at stake.

Political parties, including the Nepali Congress and the communists, were swooping in. The king's popularity dipped, then plummeted. The youths stepped onto the streets, screaming angry slogans, demanding democracy and an end to monarchy.

Eleven years on, the same men would shave their heads, wail on the roads and beat their chests, shouting 'Come back King, save the country.'

But for now, violent protests swept through the nation as the Nepali Congress and the communists mounted a string of protests. Nepal became a constitutional monarchy with a multiparty Parliament, but the success came with a price: a forty-nine-day struggle left approximately 500 people dead. Bhattarai was sworn in as the first prime minister of the constitutional monarchy era and supervised the drafting of the country's new constitution and Parliament elections.

It was one of Nepal's biggest ironies: Girija Prasad Koirala, the man who now took King Birendra's position as Nepal's elected administrator, was the youngest brother of B.P. Koirala, the man whom the monarch's father had humiliated, sacked and arrested thirty years ago.

When the king had abdicated absolute power, retaining direct control only over the army, monarchy seemed passing through its worst phase in Nepal. But as democracy came into its own after 1990, it faltered. The politicians turned out to be poor administrators.

Over the next few years, allegations of corruption, misrule and red tape followed. Successive governments took over, cracked and collapsed in a massive game of Russian roulette that seemed to always throw up one big question: Had Nepal's gamble with democracy gone all wrong? Was the absolute monarch a better bet than the elected prime minister?

The fledgling democracy had failed to live up to the people's expectations. As the politicians faltered, the king began to win back points he had lost over the years in the pro-democracy campaign. He had behind him two of the most powerful forces in Nepal—the reverence for the monarchy, and the royal army. But he played with honesty, courage and conviction the role of constitutional monarch that he had given himself. King Birendra, who had completed three decades on the throne shortly before his death, proved that even in a kingdom as traditional as Nepal, a middle way could be found between monarchy and democracy, and that constitutional monarchy could be a reality.

He did not give in to demands that he should take over the control of the nation once again. The demands had continued until weeks before his killing, when the Rashtriya Prajatantra Party, the country's third largest, urged a royal takeover as the government struggled with a scandal over the lease of a jetliner belonging to Austria's Lauda Air.

Forty years after King Mahendra carried out the *coup de grace* in 1960 to usurp power, King Birendra could have carried out a similar task with ease, with the army at his control. He had recurring examples of other army takeovers before him within the region—in Pakistan and Bangladesh.

But King Birendra remained true to his word. He never crossed the line.

The democracy movement of 1990 had also put in a corner the mainline communist movement, which had started in 1949. All included, soon there would be four dozen communist parties in the country. But the veteran communist leaders were confronted during the late 1980s by a wave of young, passionate, impatient activists and leaders, who wanted action, not words—and sooner, rather than later. When the frontline communist leaders could not make the radical moves that the firebrands wanted, the young leaders left the parties. The liberals among the communists remained in the United Left Front. The new grouping formed a rival bloc, loosely called The Radicals.

In a nation where the population profile is relatively young—people over sixty-five years form just 3 per cent of the population, and the next generation, of people up to fourteen years, form a whopping 41 per cent—the young people's voice had to be heard. The biggest revolution of Nepalese youth was under way.

The young communist leaders slammed and rejected the nation's new constitution, accepted in 1990 by the king and the new government. Two young leaders, Nirmal Lama and Pushpa Kumar Dahal, started the underground Unity Centre. In 1996, Dahal branched off and set up his own Communist Party of Nepal, and declared war on the government and the monarchy with a band of ill-equipped but fiercely loyal cadres. He claimed support among many of the ethnic groups that form Nepal's society.

Years passed. The revolution spread. The sound of conch shells was echoing across the mountains. Only, they were not being used to offer salutations to the gods; rebel leaders were using them to summon their cadres to torchlight meetings. There were war cries against the government and the monarchy. They sent chills down a thousand spines.

Within a few years, the Maoists already seemed threatening enough to pose a real threat to Nepal's democracy. They frequently overran and burned down police stations, snatched police weapons, and mercilessly killed policemen. The campaign made quick progress. The rebels now run their independent administration in five of the country's 73 districts, and have influence of varying degrees in 73 of 75 districts. Of these, they have carried out killings in 58 districts. At last count, more than 1,700 people had died in the five-year insurgency. The targets of the Maoists have included the workers of non-governmental groups, including American organizations like CARE. But the Maoists have remained in the shadows: little more is known about them and estimates of the armed Maoist cadres vary from 3,000 to 20,000.

The Maoist weaponry includes crude guns, or those snatched from the police, khukris—traditional Nepalese daggers—and truncheons. They normally move in large groups, often up to 200 guerrillas attacking terrified policemen in a single post, or snatching land documents from banks and government offices and burning down the buildings.

The Maoists draw inspiration from Shining Path guerrillas, who fought a similar war in rural Peru in the 1980s and the early 1990s. Like the Peruvian rebels, Nepal's Maoists are led by educated leaders once counted among intellectuals within the communist leadership.

The Maoists are believed to have close links with communist rebels in Peru, the Philippines and in the Indian states of Andhra Pradesh and Bihar, where left-wing rebels run a ruthless terror campaign in several areas.

Within Nepal, they enjoy tremendous support in several rural stretches where poverty shows up at its worst, but have little following in the towns and cities. Hundreds of Maoist workers help local people run development and construction projects, plant and harvest crops, and have a system of administration that is based on equal access to environmental resources for all people in their territories. Maoist courts dispense tough and quick justice.

But the Maoists also face allegations of human rights violations. Human rights groups including Amnesty International say there is evidence that the guerrillas are increasingly employing boys and girls as young as fourteen, and abducting innocent civilians in their fight against the Nepalese police. Many children were abducted from their schools. The rebels also reportedly use excessive torture as a powerful weapon in their campaign. Those suspected of being informers or having links with the police are killed or crippled by having their legs broken by heavy boulders. The police are also accused of misusing their powers, including torturing people to force confessions, and killing civilians in anti-Maoist operations.

Some peace moves had taken place between the Maoists and the government during the lifetime of King Birendra. The first attempts were made in 1997. They failed. Both sides were too rigid for any forward movement to take place; the Maoists had even placed a condition that the government formally declare their seventy-two dead comrades as martyrs. The government prodded them again in January 1999, forming a committee to engage the rebels in talks. The guerrillas refused. In March 2000, Prachanda agreed to talk, but with forty conditions, and to deal with any party except the Nepali Congress.

For the monarch, the good news was that the Maoists slammed the monarchy but never made personal attacks against him. The Maoists regarded King Birendra as a true Nepali nationalist. In another of Nepal's quaint ironies, Prachanda would send a message of tribute hailing the death of the king whose monarchy he had set out to destroy.

King Birendra had another quality that might have endeared him to the Maoist rebels: his inability to take tough decisions. As an administrator, his biggest fault seemed to be his indecisiveness. He sometimes preferred to pass on to the Supreme Court controversial matters on which he had to take a decision; acts described as maturity by some, and prevarication by others. He had become a laid-back monarch.

He rarely spoke out his mind on affairs of the state, always bearing in mind that the most innocuous of his remarks could have a deep impact. But in a rare comment before diplomats at a 2000 dinner, he was quoted as saying by the *Nepali Times* weekly: 'Only if people in responsible positions carry out their duties with care and accountability and treat all Nepalese equally, will the people of this country believe completely in democracy.'

As the Maoist rebellion gained pace, King Birendra was hemmed in by demands from political parties to deploy the Royal Nepal Army to fight the rebels. It was a decision only he could take as the supreme commander of the armed forces. It was well known that the Nepalese soldiers were loyal to the palace rather than the government, and the king did not want the army to get sucked into an insurgency. He wanted to avoid pushing his army into a situation similar to that in India, where troops were fighting an endless war against Islamic guerrillas in Kashmir and several rebel groups in the north-eastern hills.

But sharp differences had emerged between the palace and the government over the issue as police casualties rose sharply. As dozens of Maoist guerrillas attacked a police post in a night swoop in late 2000, an army camp nearby ignored the policemen's SOS for help, provoking the then interior minister and the prime minister's powerful confidante, Govind Raj Joshi, to angrily quit his post.

King Birendra soon announced the formation of an armed police force numbering around 15,000 to fight the Maoists, but still did not opt for the army's deployment. He also rejected and sent for review a Parliament ordinance giving sweeping powers to the police to search vehicles and homes of people suspected to have Maoist links. The indecision won him praise from the guerrillas themselves, who interpreted it as the king's reluctance to turn the army on what they call the people's war.

Nepal's army remains its holy cow, second only to the palace in its stature. Headquartered in Kathmandu, it is patterned after the British and Indian armies, with which it has had close links. Nepal does not have an air force, but the army runs an air wing. The most well known part of the army are the fierce Gurkhas, who have excelled in several international peacekeeping missions and are wooed also by the Indian and the British armies. The elite Royal Guards Brigade exclusively serves the royal family and palace. Brigades stationed in and around Kathmandu also include the signals, engineer, artillery, transport and medical units, as well as the airborne Para Battalion. Nepalese soldiers remain poorly equipped compared to their counterparts in the region, but they are among the best.

The king's powerful hold on the royal army spilled over to his family too. Many members of the royal family were honorific officers in the army. Crown Prince Dipendra himself received formal military training. He was a colonel-in-chief in the army, who used his authority to freely take weapons from the royal armoury in the Narayanhiti Palace. These included lethal assault rifles, pistols and other weapons. He loved weapons: photographs of the crown prince admiring an automatic rifle in a military ordnance factory in Wah, Pakistan, would be emblazoned in newspapers for weeks after his death.

On most days, he shot monkeys, cats and other animals within the palace compounds in his target practice. One day, he changed his mind.

Chapter Three

A Prince in Love

THE NOISY PARTY was warming up at the residence
of a royal family relative in 1995. Several young people
got up to dance. One of them, a heavily built youth of
about twenty-four, was keenly watching a stunningly
beautiful woman at the other end of the room.

The young man wanted a dance with her. Confident,
specially as he knew her, he walked up.

'Can I have a dance?' he asked.

'Thank you, but no thank you, Your Highness . . .
my parents do not allow me to dance with anyone but
my brother,' the lady said, as she brushed off the
request with a charming smile.

Dipendra—who had once told a British friend that
'I am the crown prince and no woman can say no to
me'—was floored.

This was no ordinary woman. She was Devyani
Rana, who would become the crown prince's beloved
years later.

In ordinary circumstances, it would be an occasion
for festivity in the royal household, and she would
become the darling of the royal household, but this was
different. The queen had always had different ideas

about the girl whom her eldest son would marry.

But Dipendra wanted to make Devyani his mother's successor as the Queen of Nepal. The thought had first crossed his mind when he saw her almost a decade ago in Britain, at the home of his local guardian, Lord Camoys, during a party. The family was very close to the royal family ever since Lord Camoys was asked by the British Foreign Office to travel to Nepal and help King Birendra prepare for Eton, where he went in 1959. Lord Camoys's son was Dipendra's best friend at Eton. Devyani was visiting London with her father, who was then a government minister.

They met, and while Devyani probably thought nothing of it, Dipendra, even then, was bowled over.

The crown prince would tell his friends later: 'When I first saw her, I told myself: she's fit to be the queen of Nepal.'

It was an innocuous remark. They drifted away.

Years later, when Dipendra returned to Nepal after completing his studies, they started communicating again, by default. The crown prince became a good friend of Urvashi, the elder sister of Devyani. When he called Urvashi, her younger sister often picked up the phone. Dipendra and Devyani also became friends.

And for almost three years now, they were very much in love, meeting every day, talking on the telephone several times, and, like any pair of young lovers, seeking secret rendezvous. Dipendra had now decided to get married to the woman he loved, whether his parents agreed or not.

The decision was guided by love—but not just. The crown prince's life had revolved around a clutch of aims he had clung to: *Proving himself. Seeking acceptance.*

Reaching out. They had made him a split personality.

Dipendra had nurtured some of these qualities since the first day when he stepped into the Kanti Ishwori Children's School wearing the school uniform of a grey shirt, maroon trousers and a grey sweater. He was just three years old—chubby-cheeked, naughty, and, for the first time, stepping out to mix with ordinary children outside the palace. The year was 1974.

Royal ADCs in plainclothes accompanied him every day as he was driven to the school building at Tripureshwor. Two years ago, at the age of one, he had already been declared the heir apparent to the throne. The trappings of power and regal grandeur set him apart from the other schoolboys.

That is, only as long as he was in the car.

Once out of it, he raced to his pre-nursery classroom and his friends, clutching his bag. The ADCs went inside the campus and walked the crown prince to his classroom. Then they left, to wait elsewhere in the campus until the session ended.

In the school building, Dipendra became part of the noisy, chaotic classroom.

To his classmates, Dipendra was just the fun-loving friend who brought boiled eggs and sandwiches in his lunch box and shared them with his friends in the break—as he grabbed others' food as well. His passion for food would follow him all his life.

On the playground, Dipendra played as enthusiastically as any of the other children. Sometimes one of the ADCs would step forward and bar the children from playing too rough—only to face an imploring crown prince.

When it was Parents' Day, their guardians would

stream into the school to watch the children draw, paint, act and dance. At the head of the crowds were Dipendra's parents, the king and the queen, proudly watching their son.

By the time he reached the second grade, Dipendra had started learning to be a leader. He began by becoming the captain of the school's scout team.

At the age of eight, in 1979, Dipendra left the school. He had reached the third grade, where he secured the first division. By that time, the school had other royal children as well: Princess Shruti, Prince Nirajan, and Prince Paras, son of King Birendra's younger brother, Prince Gyanendra.

It was also around this time that the sensitive boy received as a birthday gift, from his family, the first of his lethal playthings: a 9 mm pistol. His parents seemed to want him to become more manly, stronger and ruthless in a conventional sense—a little too early in life.

Dipendra's fingers had until now handled only pencils, paint brushes and soccer balls; now they were thrust on a trigger. The crown prince's family had set the innocent child on a dangerous path.

Meanwhile, he also nurtured his precious innocence. He would miss two of his schools all his life. The first was Kanti Ishwori; the second was the Budhanilkantha High School, where he now went. The Budhanilkantha boarding school for boys had been set up jointly by the governments of Britain and Nepal as part of education reforms in the country.

When King Birendra decided to send his son to these schools, he had faced strong opposition from conservatives in the royal family. Many relatives argued that the crown prince should not be sent to a school where he would study with commoners. Some suggested that Dipendra study in separate classes where he would remain segregated from the king's subjects. The king laughed off the objections.

Dipendra stayed at Budhanilkantha, which literally means 'the old kingfisher', for seven years. The school drew its name from a nearby shrine to Lord Vishnu, where thousands thronged each year. Ironically, a quaint tradition barred Nepal's king from visiting the shrine.

The school helped him grow tremendously as a person. These early years in many ways shaped one part of his lifelong personality. The other part was shaped by his parents, especially his mother.

His new classmates at Budhanilkantha saw him as 'brilliant but lazy'. Dipendra was always very sharp in class, grasping his lessons very quickly. His favourite subjects were history and geography—and he was a little scared of maths.

The school also laid the foundation of his passion for sports. He loved tennis, squash, golf and especially soccer—playing as a defender, from which position he loved to send the ball soaring across the field with some hard kicks. Very soon, he was playing for the Budhanilkantha soccer team in the national school-level competitions.

When he was not in the classroom or on the playgrounds, Dipendra could be found in the school auditorium. He loved to act in plays, and his peers would remember several of his performances for years. There he was, among the leading nobles in Julius Caesar and Macbeth. He loved to play king. He loved to play pauper. One of Dipendra's most memorable roles during his schooldays was of a pavement dweller in a play called *Sadak Dekhi Sadak Samm* (From Road to Road). It was a real-life look at the situation of the country in all its poverty and squalor, and the life of its people, from the point of view of a person sitting on a pavement. The play won the first prize in the Inter-Valley School competition for single-act plays.

With accolades, came punishment. Like all other students, Dipendra too was sometimes punished for indiscipline, or not doing the homework, and for bullying other students. There were two forms of punishment which students detested the most.

The first was fashionably called 'Ten Past Six'. It was nice-sounding only in name: students had to get up at dawn and assemble at 6:10 a.m., when they were subjected to punishment accumulated from the previous day. Drowsy students got up from their cosy beds to go to the playground and cut grass and perform other menial jobs. Dipendra was among those punished more than once. The other punishment was detention in the classroom, where students had to study for an hour after school behind closed doors.

Dipendra did not mind the punishment. He loved the school. He loved the teachers. His favourites were John Tyson, the principal, Rambabu Subedi and Dharmapal Thapa, the history teacher. Before Thapa started teaching, the students hated history. But he made it so interesting that it became the favourite subject of most boys.

But Thapa was an officer of the Royal Nepalese Army who would become commander-in-chief—what was he doing here, teaching history at a British-run school?

Thapa was among several decoy teachers at the Budhanilkantha—all of them senior army officers—who were given employment, drawing salaries from both the school and the palace. Their main task was to keep a sharp eye on the security of the crown prince, without anyone knowing and any school activity getting disturbed. The officers had found the perfect way to spend their time at the school constructively, even when they maintained their cloak of anonymity: they became teachers!

Dipendra stayed at the school until 1987, when he wrote his School Leaving Certificate examinations. The last few weeks before the examinations were full of the pangs of leaving their cherished school, and the excitement of heading for new avenues. By this time, Dipendra was the 10th grade prefect, and the student-in-charge of his Pumori Hostel, one of the several school hostels named after a mountain.

Dipendra and his friends studied until late in the night for the examinations. They had kept a heater in the room that was used to make tea when they started to drop off to sleep. There was a problem though: they often got hungry during the nights—the crown prince leading the way—long after the fixed hours of the school mess were over and there was no chance of getting even a crumb of bread until the morning.

Hunger was the great unifier for many students. Days were fixed in the hostel mess for serving separate dishes. In the eyes of the hostelers, the most popular day, for which each student waited for a whole week, was the Chicken Day, when they would be served a chicken dish. Like all hostel students starved of home-cooked food, this day was sacred. In Dipendra's Pumori

Hostel, many students skipped dinner the previous night and even did heavy workouts in the gym so that they would be very, very hungry when they walked into the mess on Chicken Day.

So on those nights during the examinations, when the pangs of hunger became unbearable, the choice for Dipendra and his gang was clear.

Beg. Borrow. Steal.

A column of young and hungry soldiers—all students of the 10th class—used to steal out of the hostel building in the dead of night, walking silently past the guard, across the campus to the mess building. Within minutes, they were swarming the kitchen, looking for whatever was left from dinner, and begging the kitchen staff for food. If threats, bribes and requests failed to work with the regulation-bound staff—no problem.

The students turned back, walked out, and returned when the staff was asleep.

His love for food and his endearing gluttony seems to have earned him a nickname from his friends: Elephant.

The magic of the hostel life at Budhanilkantha, which taught Dipendra the virtues of independence, bonding and sharing, ended in 1987. He made a small circle of friends with whom he would remain in touch all his life. Even when driving around in his Land Cruiser, he would stop by the roadside if he saw a classmate and chat about old times. When he was abroad, if he met a youth who had studied at Budhanilkantha, he would ask him out to dinner and talk about the school and the teachers for long hours.

Dipendra had asked his younger brother and sister to break protocol and address his friends as 'Dai',

Nepalese for elder brother. It was a huge gesture: normally, those who get the opportunity to interact with the royalty have to use a formal form of address. The members of the royal family have to be addressed as 'Your Highness', and the national dress has to be worn when meeting them.

For example, when someone is meeting the king, one cannot say: 'Your Majesty, I wish to start this project to raise awareness about AIDS.' The correct sentence would be: 'Your Majesty, your humble subject seeks your kind permission to start this project to raise awareness about AIDS in your kingdom.'

No such thing for Dipendra.

In 1995, the principal of the Kanti Ishwori School was on the phone one evening, frantically calling up the numbers of all the old students he could gather. The crown prince had called up the school, saying he wanted to come the next day with Princess Shruti, where they would witness an invocation to Saraswati, the goddess of learning, and meet old classmates.

Only six students could be informed. The crown prince did not mind.

'It's been a long time since we met. Let's keep in touch,' he told them. Then he suggested that they form an alumni association, and pointed to one of his former classmates.

'Why don't you take charge?' he said.

Within weeks, 'Friends of KISB' was registered. It had four life members—Crown Prince Dipendra, Princess Shruti, Prince Nirajan and Prince Paras.

The membership of three of those was to end soon.

Dipendra took a keen interest in activities of the alumni association, encouraging its members to organize frequent meetings and events, including music competitions, school fairs, blood donation camps and tree plantation ceremonies. He would sometimes drive to the association's meetings in the Kanti Ishwori campus. And later in 2001, he was going to be on the board of the Budhanilkantha School.

Dipendra also invited, with an unfailing regularity, several of his old school friends to an annual reception held on his birthday, 27 June, in a sprawling hall in the royal palace, where his young schoolmates rubbed shoulders with ambassadors, government ministers and other top officials.

In 1987, it was time to spread his wings farther. The crown prince travelled to Eton College in Windsor, England, to complete his 'O' and 'A' levels. He was accompanied by his ADCs. He was ready to see a whole new side of life. The boy was ready to become a man.

As in his previous two schools, Dipendra did not take too long to make new friends. He became well known during his stay there between 1987 and 1990. Sometimes it was for the right reasons; sometimes for the wrong ones.

Nicknamed 'Dippy' by his friends, the crown prince evoked curiosity and some awe among his British classmates. The reasons were many: his regal background; his apparent grandeur back home; his colourful stories of the nation often known in the West as a quaint Oriental kingdom; and his loaded revolver—another of the weapons that had become a habit for him by now. According to his former classmates, Dipendra kept the revolver in his room.

At Eton, he remained bright in studies. He loved partying, gossiping, and making new friends. One of the enduring images of Dipendra at Eton would be the sight of him on the soccer ground during the Eton Field Game, bathed in mud, his socks drooping down to his ankles and his back straight and chest puffed in defiance. Dipendra also loved to be naughty: a classmate was quoted in media reports as saying that he would sometimes scamper down corridors, banging on students' doors and frightening them.

On weekends, Dipendra sometimes drove to the barracks of the Gurkha soldiers at the Sandhurst Military Academy, and drew them into dance and songs. As Dipendra played the traditional instrument called the 'madal'—which he excelled at—the soldiers clapped, danced and sang with him.

The qualities which endeared a complete stranger to the crown prince were soon clear to his classmates at Eton as well. He was down-to-earth and without airs in his immediate circle. He also had a great sense of humour.

Always quick to make friends, Dipendra, at nineteen, walked one day wearing his combat jacket into a boutique called Skin Appeal in Windsor during his final year. Twenty-year-old Rossella Scarcella, an Italian girl, was at the counter. He rummaged for a long time through clothes and costume jewellery, and Rossella was beginning to wonder if the scruffy boy would ever make up his mind. But Dipendra soon chose a leather jacket and walked up to the counter to make the payment. She noticed the words HRH—'His Royal Highness'—before his name. Dipendra then told her, in a matter-of-fact way, that he was the crown prince of Nepal. Rossella and Dipendra were friends soon, and the crown prince loved to play with her Yorkshire terrier, Yuppie. He was back soon, and Rossella, who had only recently arrived from Florence, went for walks with the crown prince by the river, during which they had long chats.

'Tell me about your love life . . . do you have anyone in mind?' Rossella once asked him on one of their walks.

'I am looking,' he said, and smiled.

'Will you have an arranged marriage?' she asked.

'Yes. I'll go through with it but it would be much better if love was involved,' Dipendra replied.

Apart from yearning for love like any other young man, Dipendra had other things on his mind. He was trying to fulfill his royal responsibilities even when he was at Eton. A fax machine in his room was his key link with his office, and he used it so much that the paper roll was changed at least twice a day. It was difficult because he was juggling his responsibilities with his 'A' level examinations.

He often told his friends he missed home, although he was happy with the complete freedom he had in England, where he wasn't bound by duties and obligations. But even there, he had not given up on his old friends at the Budhanilkantha School.

Dipendra's friends there often got together during lunch breaks to read letters from England with a hasty scrawl inside reporting all things important and sundry, from frivolous teenage gossip to yarns of Eton days to messages about his yearning for his country.

There was no name written in the space for the sender's identity on the envelopes.

There was just the sketch of an elephant.

Dipendra joined Eton's Combined Cadet Force, a

good training ground for his formal military training much later, at home. He also loved to participate in mock karate fights with friends in the school corridors, and would became head of Eton's martial arts society.

Back home he was also set to achieve greater power, in a different sense: in December 1988, the coming of age ceremony of the crown prince was celebrated. He was elevated to the status of a god.

After his return to Eton, this meant that he would henceforth be exempted from attending chapel, since one god did not have to worship another. One of his friends quoted him as reacting thus to this decision by the college authorities: 'Yes I am a god now, but the main thing is always what you feel inside, not what people say about you. It is up to all of us to prove that we are special.'

All his life, he had proved that he was special. But he also started doing things at Eton that ordinary mortals did.

Like many young men his age, he started experimenting with alcohol and drugs. His royal background and the mystique associated with him gave enough fodder to British tabloids to splash the scandal on their front pages, bringing embarrassment to the king and queen. The worst came when he was caught selling liquor, apparently brought by his ADCs, to other students. He was confined to his room by school authorities for several days and was fined eight pounds.

Some palace officials say the ADCs shielded and encouraged the habits. It was not unusual to find whisky bottles scattered in his room.

Dipendra took a break from studies in January 1990, to take part in one of the most important royal events for a crown prince. At a grand ceremony at the Narayanhiti Palace, King Birendra conferred on the crown prince the title of Colonel-in-Chief of the Royal Nepalese Army and offered him the royal dagger, the symbol of a full colonel.

Dipendra left Eton in July 1990 with three 'A' level grades. Classmates had mixed memories of him. Some of his classmates feared him, and would later describe him as a 'dark, sullen' character. At times, they said, he was a loner, often intimidating.

His classmate Daniel Kruger once teased him when Dipendra was doing skipping exercises in the school gymnasium. Kruger says Dipendra got upset and lifted him off the ground by his jaw.

'He said: "Don't laugh at me. Don't ever laugh at me,"' Kruger said. 'I felt quite threatened.' One of the people who would miss him the most would be Tom Holden, his housemaster, who reared him with great affection. Holden had tutored King Birendra as well, and had also looked after Dipendra at his residence.

In Nepal, King Birendra seemed ready to groom his son for a greater role in his kingdom.

But the nation's destiny itself was about to change.

The revolution was already brewing when Dipendra landed at the Tribhuvan International Airport on 14 July 1990. As winter approached, it had intensified, with tens of thousands of youths coming out on the streets and clashing with the police, as they screamed slogans against the same king they had revered for decades.

Once King Birendra gave up power, life changed for Dipendra. The crown prince of the Nepal ruled by the Shah dynasty and the crown prince of the constitutional monarchy were two different people. These were trying times for Nepal's monarchy. Unlike in the past, it was not fashionable to be a royalist any more. The monarchy seemed jaded. The glitter was gone.

Dipendra soon realized that he would have little responsibility in any affairs of the state and the palace for a long time. Over the next decade, it would become one of his most nagging frustrations.

He started focussing on things he liked most in life. To begin with, it meant pursuing studies and living up to his father's expectations. He enrolled for a Bachelor of Arts course at the Traichandra campus at Kathmandu's Tribhuvan University.

Devyani, meanwhile, had enrolled in the prestigious Lady Sriram College in Delhi. She had finished her studies in two of the finest schools in the country—the Rishi Valley School and the Welham Girls'. Devyani was one of the best students in her class, as also one of the most reclusive. Devyani specialized in international relations and was also very politically aware. She started a thorough study of Nepalese politics, inspired by the tumultuous events that had taken place in her country with the return of democracy and the end of the absolute monarchy.

Devyani made a conscious attempt to keep a low profile and hated flaunting her royal lineage. When she was asked by her teachers once to help get Madhavrao Scindia, her uncle, to be the chief guest at a college function, she had said: 'Yes, I will, but on one condition: it will not be disclosed why he agreed to come and who the contact person is.' She was not too keen to participate in any college activities other than her studies.

In Nepal, his father had already declared Dipendra

a colonel-in-chief, but he wanted to earn his title. In 1991, he became the first crown prince of Nepal to enrol for the Officers' Cadet Basic Training course at the Royal Nepalese Military Academy at Kharipati. He would soon supplement his skills with a Commando Warfare Course.

These were unusual decisions for a royal family member—most of whom had so far earned honorific military titles, and had never undergone military training with the troops. Dipendra had to shed all his regal grandeur and don fatigues. He had to bear bruised knees and grimy clothes, tough drills, impossible deadlines, and mix with ordinary soldiers. He passed out the same year, now a real soldier.

Years later, his friends would remark at his ability never to back away from a challenge or fight: part of his smugness came from the fact that he was a fifth Dan black belt in karate.

Meanwhile, he also maintained his bright academic record, graduating in 1992 with a first division. Dipendra had a keen interest in geography, and he now wanted to specialize in the subject. He started studying for a Masters Degree in geography, and passed out in 1994. He topped the university in both the B.A. and M.A. courses. What next? He wanted a doctorate, and signed up for an advanced course in political demography at the Department of Population.

Dipendra revived old friendships. He sought out old acquaintances—including Devyani, who had passed out from Lady Sriram College in 1993 and returned to Nepal. For many years, they would just remain friends.

Dipendra loved sitting with friends talking until late into the night, when many of them would shed protocol and address him by his nickname—'CP', short form for his official status. At such meetings with friends, Dipendra loved his drink and gossip about old times, enjoying the special togetherness that the friends had shared. His friends looked up to him also because he was an ideal drinker: he could drink all night and yet never blab, quarrel, stammer, slur or abuse. When it seemed to him that he could go out of control, he would put down his glass and say coolly: 'It's time to stop.' And if he had had several drinks, he asked his ADC to drive.

To his friends and cousins, it was a glimpse of another of the qualities they admired in him: his strong, indestructible will power.

According to his close relatives, Dipendra sometimes used drinking as a tool to gain wider acceptance among his peers and common people. He wanted to seem like them. So he had to be more like them.

But in many respects, Dipendra could be more of a commoner than his friends. He loved rural entertainment, Nepalese music and rustic food.

While in school, Dipendra had mastered a fascinating Nepalese form of community singing called *Dohri Geet*— double songs—in which two teams of a few members each are formed to sing and compete against each other. All the songs are set to one tune, which can play for hours while the contest continues. It is a very difficult art to master, because singers have to sing a song, then hear the rivals sing, and meanwhile compose a new song to retort to the rivals' lines. On his treks into remote areas or visits to military cantonments, he often walked into army barracks and, before the soldiers could spring to their feet, challenged them to a round of

Dohri Geet. Most of the lines he created were songs of hardship, of ordinary lives, and of togetherness in difficult times. It was a great way to establish camaraderie with the army soldiers. The crown prince often amazed listeners with his ability to excel in this game in which one had to be a singer, lyricist and a quick thinker, all rolled into one.

Besides songs, he also wrote poems. Dipendra was passionately interested in the Nepalese language and literature. Words had a deep meaning for him. He studied the origin of many words, and the dialects in which they were spoken. On some days, he would appear cheerfully before friends or young cousins, flip out a piece of paper from his pocket and start reading lines from a new poem.

Then he would pause and say: 'Hey guys, what do you think of it?'

Most of Dipendra's poems were shared with his closest friends, who treasure them too much to make them public. But a few have been published. The following are a few lines from a translated poem titled 'Soldier':

> *My bonds of affection are ripped away. I know now.*
> *If asked to fight, soaked in blood, I will now . . .*
> *To douse these flames, to halt this lightning, I will spray my blood*
> *In this uniform, the vermilion of my nation, I will shake the Earth . . .*

Dipendra had a strong grasp over Nepalese, in which he mostly wrote. According to a source close to him, the crown prince was inspired by all the great poets of Nepal, as also his grandfather, King Mahendra, and his mother, Queen Aiswarya.

Dipendra's poetry spoke of nationalism and romance, and he took his analogies from the breathtaking natural beauty of the country, its diverse art and culture and centuries-old history. For his upcoming thirtieth birthday, he had planned to publish a collection of his poems, as his mother, grandmother, and his uncle, Prince Gyanendra, had done in the past.

Dipendra also enjoyed reading English poetry and literature, especially the works of Shakespeare, and the poetry of Robert Browning, John Donne, and Andrew Marvell. He knew many poems by heart and sometimes quoted from them.

A passion for music was entwined with his love for writing poetry. Dipendra thrived on Nepalese music. He loved hearing on his music system vintage and new songs, and, at the other end of the musical spectrum, classical Western music. When not listening to his favourite songs, Dipendra played on the piano and the electric guitar.

Along with his creative adventures in music, drama and poetry, Dipendra's keen sensitivity had been shaped since childhood by religion and he was familiar with the major religious texts like the Vedas and the Bhagavad Gita.

Dipendra carefully nurtured several qualities of his father which had endeared the monarch to his people. He loved meeting people. This was also part of his preparation to gain the wide knowledge he was expected to have in different fields, like King Birendra. Once a week, Dipendra tried to meet people from different areas of life and brainstorm with them about the country and the world. Dipendra's close friends saw him as a nationalist leader on the lines of his father.

He often caught people off guard by approaching them unexpectedly. As he jogged around the royal palace in T-shirt, shorts, and dark glasses, he would start chatting with a startled pedestrian. Dipendra also seemed to enjoy creating a flutter at stiff official functions by doing something casual, or by giving a display of his keen sense of humour. And he always came across to his peers and common people as someone who was not overly conscious of his status—such as by introducing himself by his first name.

Not many people outside his circles knew that even in the palace, he sometimes sprang surprises on the staff by doing small jobs—on one day, before the arrival of a guest in the palace, he was found on top of a wooden stool, trying to fix faulty electric bulbs.

Many young people in Nepal remember a sunny December afternoon in 1995, on the king's birthday, when a massive street festival witnessed tens of thousands of youth descending on the King's Way. Among the hordes of people dancing to racy numbers, blaring on huge speakers, was a young man dressed in a jacket, jeans and a denim cap: the crown prince. The crowd started getting more raucous, and seemed set to go out of control. The organizers switched off the music, fearing a stampede.

Like any other annoyed teenager, Dipendra came running to the main organizer and asked him to switch on the music again.

'This is not fair. We are all enjoying. You are a spoilsport,' he said.

A month before his death, he was taking the round

of the Thimi Food Festival, which had drawn a huge number of visitors. As he walked past the stalls, accompanied by government ministers and ambassadors, he suddenly changed course and stopped before a stall selling Chinese food.

'Can I have some momos, please?' he asked with the yearning of a teenager clutching precious pocket money. Minutes later, he was standing before a stall selling beaten rice and other traditional Newari food, eating the food off a plate made from a large leaf. Then he took a swig of a glass of homemade brew.

One of his favourite weekend getaways was the Baithak restaurant at the posh shopping mall called Baber Mahal Revisited. The complex was recreated from a cowshed, which was all that a young descendant of the former Rana rulers got when Nepal's government took over the palace of his ancestors. Baithak prepared a special menu for the crown prince, which continues to be called the Royal Menu. It was served on a huge silver tray in ornate dishes.

Here is the menu of the typical meal that Dipendra loved at the Baithak—so much that he ordered it again after finishing it once: For starters, *Baphai ko Bandel* (Steamed wild boar), *Chara ko Kacho Bara* (Hand pounded chicken marinated with herbs and fried into fluffy balls), *Maas Daal ko Bara* (Ground black lentils deep fried into fluffy balls), *Aaloo ko Ledo Achar* (Marinated and spiced potatoes), *Chara ko Ras* (Chicken soup slowly simmered with spices); for the main course— *Basmati Kesari Bhuja* (Long grained rice simmered in saffron water and clarified butter), *Chhane ko Daal* (Yellow lentils cooked with spices and strained through muslin), *Khasi ko Korma* (Succulent cubes of mutton cooked in an aromatic tomato gravy), *Chara ko Sekuwa* (Boneless pieces of chicken marinated and charcoal grilled), *Dahi Aaloo* (Potatoes cooked in a gravy of yogurt), *Palunga ko Saag* (Spinach from the valley of Palung, sautéed in mustard oil and garlic), *Golbeda*, *Hariyo Pyaaj, Kerau Tare ko* (Tomato, green onions and peas, sautéed in mustard oil), *Lucci Puri* (Fried Nepali bread), *Kakro ko Achar* (Fresh cucumber pickle); and, for dessert, *Sikarni* (Sweet, spiced yogurt strained through muslin).

Food. Poetry. Music. That was not all. Dipendra patronized efforts to restore Nepal's heritage by raising funds for the independent Kathmandu Valley Preservation Trust. He wanted to choreograph shows of the Chhariya dancers, Buddhist performers who had perfected a dance form based on tantra that they performed in Nepal's heritage sites.

Dipendra loved modern electronic gadgets, information technology and the internet. Each time he travelled abroad, the crown prince would come back loaded with ideas on how he could develop the infotech sector in Nepal. Dipendra had planned the computerization of work at the palace, and in the army. Whenever he found the time, he would surf on the Net.

He often responded to electronic gadgets with a childlike glee. In 2000, Yogendra Sakya, one of Nepal's tourism trade leaders, mentioned to the president of Transavia, the Dutch airline, the crown prince's fetish for sophisticated electronic equipment. When the executive arrived in Nepal some time later, he had brought a two-metre miniature helicopter that flew by remote control. Dipendra loved the gadget so much that Sakya arranged for the chopper's fuel to be imported from Holland, especially for the crown prince.

A few weeks later, Sakya was at a ball presided over by the crown prince, when Dipendra walked up and greeted him. He asked Dipendra: 'Your Highness, how is the helicopter flying?'

Dipendra made a face.

'Aaah, it crashed,' he said.

The toy had crashed but Dipendra could fly a real helicopter too. In 1993, he got a private pilot's licence from the Department of Civil Aviation. He loved flying, and even pitched in with ferrying relief supplies when floods devastated parts of Nepal. In May 2000, he plunged down from an airplane, strapped to a parachute, after the completion of his course at the army's Para Training School. Soon after, he also underwent a high-risk driving course, apparently in an attempt to sharpen his knowledge about VIP security. But for most people who saw the adventurous prince zoom through Kathmandu's roads in his SUV, the crown prince did not need a course to learn high-risk driving!

The love of adventure came with his love for the countryside. Dipendra found excuses to travel outside Kathmandu to different parts of his country. Each year he spent up to a month trekking in remote areas. In a quaint throwback to his father, King Birendra's days as an avid trekker, Dipendra walked into villages, often with medicine and supplies.

Even with the tough veneer, the child in him had survived. He seemed devastated when his dog Rocky, who had been with him for fifteen years, died this year. According to Dipendra's closest friend, he felt as if he had lost a loved one. Rocky was the last in a series of pets, beginning with his stallion Damaru, whom he had trained with great affection.

However, while Dipendra retained a certain childlike innocence, he could not avoid some of the vices that came with becoming an adult. One of these was drugs.

The crown prince often smoked hashish, marijuana and other drugs, but he was not an addict who could not do without them. According to one of his closest friends: 'Whenever he smoked marijuana it made him tired and sleepy. He used to smoke it to chill out and de-stress.'

According to the friend, 'He was very very anti-hard drugs—was very insistent and never tried them, even though certain other people around him were doing it. He was very clear about what harm they could do. He even kept off any kind of allopathic medication when he had had even had one drink or smoked marijuana. He was planning to give all this up in July when he was to start his karate training.'

The occasions for having grass and other drugs were mostly weekend getaways to resorts or secret rendezvous with friends. But it was common knowledge that the youth in the royal family consumed drugs, which were sneaked into the palace by royal ADCs—and nobody seemed to mind. It was a vice that Dipendra had not been able to get rid of, for years.

It wasn't a difficult habit to maintain: the country is regarded as an illicit producer of cannabis for domestic and international drug markets and a transit point for opiates from South Asia to the West. Nor is there any taboo associated with smoking hashish and other similar drugs in the countryside. Palace staff, too, especially lower rank members, often returned from vacations in their villages and brought back hashish for an employer.

But while he was alive, Dipendra seemed too tall for scandals to touch him. He was the darling of the kingdom, who won genuine love and respect from his people. Like other members of the royal family, very little was known about his private life. But even with the little that was known, the affable prince seemed the best hope to continue the tradition of King Birendra, who had charmed his nation again after a five-year estrangement between 1990 and 1995.

Dipendra endeared himself to his country even further when he led the massive administrative effort to organize the South Asian Federation Games in 1999. It was his first major public achievement as an administrator. Dipendra put passion and hard work into the games.

They were small gestures, but they counted with the spectators. He ran along with the marathon runners to cheer and encourage them, and when Nepal won a football match against India, the crown prince walked into the field to congratulate the two teams. The entire stadium was on its feet.

'Long live the crown prince!' they screamed. Then they burst into the national anthem.

A gruelling cross-country run saw many runners taking part in the scorching heat, and when they approached the finish line, the exhausted winner fainted. The crown prince, watching from the flanks, rushed forward and held the falling runner in his arms. As water was brought, he sprinkled it on the runner's face, reviving him.

When he was not at his casual best in sporting events, Dipendra was preparing for his more serious public life as a king during his various visits to other countries, and in his interaction with top dignitaries.

During 1994, he travelled to Thailand, India and China on state visits. An official visit of Britain came three years later, in 1997. In the next year, he was in Pakistan and the Netherlands. He also represented his father abroad at several royalty-related events, including the coronation of Emperor Akihito of Japan on 12 November 1990, six days after King Birendra abdicated absolute power; in 1993, the funeral in April of Don Juan de Bozbon, the father of Spain's King Juan Carlos; and the funeral of King Boudouin of Belgium in August. He travelled to Spain again in 2000 for the funeral of King Carlos, and to Lesotho in the same year for the wedding of King Letsie III.

In 1998, he hosted Prince Charles of Britain—an occasion for him to remember his days at Eton, which, he said, gave him a sense of 'fairplay and discipline'.

In November 1999, he was in Brussels to attend the wedding reception of Crown Prince Philippe and Princess Mathilde. Dipendra was part of a glittering ceremony where he was among members of royal families from across the world, including Queen Margrethe of Denmark, King Carl-Gustav of Sweden and Queen Silvia, Prince Hans Adam of Liechtenstein, King Harald of Norway and Queen Sonja, Prince Albert of Monaco, The Prince of Wales, Crown Prince Willem-Alexander of the Netherlands and Crown Prince Naruhito of Japan.

The crown prince's last foreign visit was to Japan between 25 April and 2 May, a month before his death. Dipendra was feted there by the emperor and empress, and he met with the Japanese crown prince and other members of the royal family. King Birendra studied in

Japan in 1967, and the crown prince had visited Japan three times during his tenure. Dipendra, who learnt karate in Japan, also got the opportunity to visit two karate organizations and meet with his karate guru, Yohara.

Dipendra was planning to have a demonstration match with Yohara in November 2001, at the inauguration of the regional karate championships. He planned to begin training from the first week of July—and he promised Devyani it would begin with a conscious attempt to reduce weight. The signs were alarming: on 31 May, a day before the palace massacre, the medical reports had come in for a series of tests that Dipendra had undergone.

He had extremely high blood pressure and cholesterol, and was alarmed by his weight problem—for which Devyani also lovingly teased him.

He told one of his closest friends: 'From next week, I will be off cigarettes, off alcohol, and I will begin training for my guruji. I must lose my weight.'

And away from his public life, there was one part of him that was known for years only to a few. Love.

Dipendra, Nepal's most eligible bachelor, had a childhood sweetheart. At the age of fifteen, when the crown prince was studying in the Budhanilkantha School, Supriya Shah was the only girl outside his family whom Dipendra had interacted with. They clicked. As adolescents do, they fell in love and remained in teenage bliss. After he was eighteen and had his coming of age ceremony, Dipendra wanted to get married to Supriya. But Queen Aiswarya refused, asking him to wait.

The pro-democracy revolution took place in the next year, and the standoff between Dipendra and his mother over Supriya continued, for almost six years, as Dipendra returned from Eton and enrolled for a graduation course at the local university.

Gradually, they fell out of love. But Supriya would remain a friend.

In 1995, Devyani's elder sister Urvashi was married into the wealthy Khemka family in India. Shortly before this wedding, her parents started considering a groom for their younger daughter as well. They reportedly sent a proposal for the crown prince to the king and queen, unaware that their daughter was already a close friend of Dipendra. But the queen shrugged off the proposal, saying she was not in a hurry to get her son married.

On her own, even Devyani was not in a hurry to get married.

Devyani's former teacher, Rena Sewak, recalls a 1995 conversation with her pupil during her vacation in Kathmandu. Sewak inquired casually whether she planned to get married soon. Devyani laughed it off, jokingly blaming her aristocratic circle.

'Oh Ma'am, there is no chance of getting married here yet. One's life is so protected . . . it's not like Delhi where we could go to Connaught Place or Greater Kailash whenever we wanted,' she said. 'One can only go anywhere with our parents, and that too to our family friends' places.'

However, within a few years, the process to shortlist a bride for Dipendra had started. Queen Aiswarya asked her mother, Shree Rajya Lakshmi Rana, to shortlist a prospective bride. Among other families, she contacted Devyani's mother, but the match did not take place.

Unaware of all this, Dipendra had started depending heavily on Devyani, who was still a close friend and no more. For a long time, Devyani shrugged off the crown prince's romantic overtures. But when she did give in, finally, she fell as hopelessly in love with him as he was with her. It was hard to say when they crossed the line from being friends to lovers, but by 1998, they were passionately involved.

In the meanwhile, Dipendra's mother was considering a young and extremely intelligent lawyer to be his prospective bride. This was Garima Rana. Owing to Queen Aiswarya's strong opposition to Devyani, she broke up with Dipendra. Dipendra dated Garima for almost four months, but they soon decided, mutually, that they were not made for each other. Dipendra realized too, that he was too deeply in love with Devyani to give up on her. He and Devyani came together again.

But not for long, if one person had her way.

Queen Aiswarya did not approve of Devyani. She strongly disliked her, not because of the kind of person she was, but because of what she perceived as Devyani's inferior lineage. To many, this was astounding. Devyani's mother belonged to one of the foremost royal families of India, and her father was a senior political leader in Nepal. But Queen Aiswarya held to her view. She sometimes raised questions about her ancestors, and even said that the Gwalior rulers, the royal family of her mother, were not from the warlike Rajput tribe, but were Brahmins, and that it was a mismatch.

Devyani was cheerful and fun-loving, in contrast to the more sober royal family.

After years of opposition, Queen Aiswarya did a surprising turnaround: since she had rejected Devyani, she wanted Dipendra to marry Supriya, the girl she had rejected as a bride years ago.

Despite his mother's opposition, Dipendra only became closer to Devyani, whom he called 'my girl'. For a long time, their relationship was clandestine, and they met secretly in the homes of friends. The crown prince was the patron of the Royal Sports Council and the Nepal Olympic Committee. According to Dipendra's close relatives, he would often go to the residence of a senior Nepalese official in the country's sports establishment under the pretext of official meetings, and stay back to meet Devyani, also a family friend of the sports official.

When Dipendra went to Sydney heading the Nepalese delegation to the Olympic Games, Devyani followed on another flight, then joined him in the same hotel.

In the two years before Dipendra's death, Devyani had been with him to his Tribhuvan Sadan residence numerous times. The queen resented this. But there was no single day during their courtship when Dipendra did not meet her. Often he would send his ADCs in his car to Devyani's residence, called Bijay Baas, where they would park outside and drive up to a side door. They would then call up Devyani on her mobile phone, and she would accompany them to meet the prince.

If Devyani went to a public function with her father, Pashupati Shumshere Rana, the crown prince would mysteriously appear at the location some time later— not to wait or talk to her publicly, but to feel connected to her by just being there. At a Golf Ball at the Soaltee Hotel, Dipendra sat restlessly at a table, surrounded by officials, when he started missing Devyani and dialled her mobile number.

Devyani took the call, smiled and chatted with him, but she could have just turned her head and talked. She was sitting just two tables away from Dipendra.

There was also, sometimes, a dramatic element to their relationship. Dipendra is said to have once gone to Devyani's residence with what was apparently a bottle of poison, and he threatened to kill himself if she did not agree to marry him.

Wedding proposals were, meanwhile, pouring in for Devyani from other royal families in India, many of whom, although they have lost their formal titles, still maintain a regal status. Royal families of Bhagalpur in eastern India, and from Jaipur and Jodhpur in the desert state of Rajasthan, had contacted the parents of Devyani and the Scindias in Gwalior, seeking her hand in marriage for their princes. A prince from Gujarat seemed the most desperate and insistent. He reportedly flew into Kathmandu and stationed himself at the Yak and Yeti, one of the country's best hotels. He had thought he would leave only after he had confirmed her acceptance. He returned a bachelor.

Gossip was spreading in the elite circles of Kathmandu, especially the aristocratic families of the Shahs and the Ranas, about the romance. But being a very private person, Devyani still avoided talking about the relationship. When a very close and dear relative asked her in jest, months ago, about it, she quietly said: 'I don't know what you are talking about.'

She was also the more mature partner of the two, and she often made it clear to the crown prince that she was ready to split up if his family was irrevocably opposed to their marriage. But for Dipendra, Devyani had become everything, and he was proud to confess it before his closest friends and cousins. He talked about her with the respect due to a wife, not the casual, jestful approach towards one of several girlfriends.

The battlelines were drawn strong and clear in the royal household over the wedding issue. Nirajan and Paras were among those who backed him. Dipendra's sister, her husband Kumar Gorakh and several other royal cousins backed Queen Aiswarya and King Birendra in their opposition to the alliance.

Defying all such opposition, Dipendra and Devyani decided to shed secrecy and started meeting publicly late last year. Even a crown prince had the right to be in love, they told themselves.

They also made up their mind to get married in the upcoming wedding season—and by all indications, it would be in defiance of the wishes of Queen Aiswarya. Dipendra had made his intentions clear approximately a year ago.

At his birthday party in the palace on 27 June 2000, he ushered his sister and the younger cousins to a corner and said: 'I don't need your consent, I am telling you this—I am going to marry the girl I love.'

Princess Shruti frowned. Dipendra pushed her away.

Word spread in close circles about Dipendra's decision. A television company producing commissioned programmes for one of the world's largest news channels had already started making preparations to make an elaborate, colourful documentary on the wedding.

But according to one of Dipendra's closest friends: 'Mentally they were already married for a year.'

She tried to calm him when his temper was frayed. He called her whenever he was under high stress—and those occasions were increasing lately. Both bought each other gifts like T-shirts, watches and a camera. She started sending home-cooked, low calorie food for him in the palace. She mothered him. When he lost his cigarette lighter, she knew exactly which pocket it would be in. If he was thinking hard and seemed worried, she would know what it was about.

In May 2000, Dipendra completed his training at the Para School of the Royal Nepalese Army and was to have his first parachute jump. Dipendra called up Devyani and said he would not undertake the jump unless Devyani cooked breakfast for him and came to the airport to feed him. She did, drove to the airport, and fed him at the VIP lounge where he was ready to take the flight. Then she drove to the banks of the Manahara River, where the crown prince landed after his jump, and they drove back together.

On leisurely evenings, Dipendra and Devyani were at Fire and Ice, an Italian restaurant with plain wooden benches and hugely popular pizzas and pasta. As the ADCs sat on another bench, the crown prince and she often enjoyed the capriciossa pizzas, lost in the crowd of mainly foreign tourists who throng the restaurant.

At a party in May, a distant relative of the royal family walked up respectfully to Dipendra and informed him that her daughter was engaged and in love.

'I too am in love,' the crown prince replied, smiling.

At another party this year at the Hyatt Hotel, the couple were seen sitting close together, like young college-going lovers, at a dance.

Dipendra was looking forward to getting married and settling down in family life. He told one of his married friends: 'You are married, you have got children. Don't you think I am fond of having children too?'

In another conversation when he was feeling low, Dipendra told a close relative of Devyani: 'Tell me what do I do? What is wrong with my girl?'

'Do I advise you as a father or as a subject, Your Majesty?' the relative asked.

'Both,' Dipendra said.

'As a subject, Your Majesty, please do whatever you desire. As a father, Your Majesty, please do what your father desires,' the relative said.

As Dipendra walked out, he turned back and smiled: 'My friend, in this day and age, be thankful that your son wants to marry a girl.' Then he laughed.

There had been three weddings in the Shah dynasty which were not smooth affairs. Dipendra's uncle, the former Prince Dhirendra Shah, the king's brother, and the former Princess Ketaki Chester, Dipendra's aunt, had both been stripped of their royal titles because they married foreigners.

But the third, and older, wedding was the one in which Dipendra found a vague parallel to his own situation. King Mahendra, Dipendra's grandfather, had been married to a Rana clan lady called Indra, who gave birth to sons Birendra, Gyanendra and Dhirendra, and daughters Shobha, Shanti and Sharada. Before her death, Indra pleaded with King Mahendra that he should marry again—and that the bride be her own younger sister, Ratna. Mahendra finally gave her the promise, and Indra died soon after. But that was just the beginning of a royal standoff.

King Tribhuvan, Mahendra's father, refused to allow the wedding. This was baffling to Mahendra, because the lady he had now chosen to be queen was in no way inferior to occupy the royal throne with him, but he

could not convince his father. Finally he defied his
father and married Ratna, who became the queen. King
Tribhuvan expressed his strong disapproval for the
wedding by leaving for India during the celebrations.
Queen Ratna Rajya Lakshmi Devi Shah is now the
queen mother of Nepal.

Dipendra knew well that public opinion—and
history—were on his side. The romance flowered.

But the frustration was growing.

Chapter Four

The Fall of a Monarch

WHAT HAVE YOU done?

It was a question a father was going to ask his son that evening, and a stunned nation was going to ask its crown prince.

The massive silver-painted iron gates at the Narayanhiti Palace opened and guards stood to attention to salute the king, queen and the crown prince as the royal motorcade drove in, past a pair of well-polished nineteenth century cannons from the era of King Surendra, a Shah dynasty ancestor.

They got off the cars and walked in, through a massive and ornately carved wooden door, twenty-four feet wide, with images of Ganesh and Lakshmi, the god and goddess of prosperity, and Saraswati, the goddess of learning and the arts.

It was a palace that constantly reminded visitors of its past.

Immaculately carved black statues of horses, lions, elephants, peacocks and fish silently watched from either side those climbing up the marbled stairs. As one entered an imposing hall, massive portraits of Shah dynasty rulers gazed down. Here they were, the stalwarts of Nepal's ruling clan, who originated in the hilly area of Gurkha, that gave to the world the legendary Gurkha soldiers. On the left side of the doorway, there were portraits of Prithvinarayan Shah, the original Shah dynasty conqueror, Pratap Singh Shah, and King Mahendra Bir Bikram Shah, who died in 1972 and was succeeded by King Birendra.

Across the hallway were huge portraits of the nineteenth century kings Rajendra Bikram Shah and Prithvi Bir Bikram Shah (1875–1911); the second king's rule marking the passage into the twentieth century. Two large photographs of King Birendra's mother, Queen Indra, and his stepmother—and the current queen mother—Queen Ratna—adorned a teak table.

A stunning wall-to-wall photograph of Mt. Everest, known in Nepal as the Sagarmatha, adorned the wall of a room to the left, probably the reason why it was called 'Parbat' (mountain). This room housed the gifts that the king had received over the years from other royal family heads and members, and visiting government leaders. Two stuffed leopards stared down at the room crammed with mementos including clocks, cups, vases, ivory carvings, plaques, certificates, statues and medals.

On the way up, there were more huge portraits. There was King Tribhuvan, the grandfather of King Birendra, and his ancestors King Surendra, King Rajendra and King Prithvi Bir. The walls were also decorated with the trophies these kings had brought back from their hunting trips in the thick forests of Nepal. There were two stuffed tigers, standing on their hind legs like intimidating doormen, watched by two heads of jealous rhinos, looming over the hallway, and a much-envied gift of a pair of ivory tusks, each at least five feet long.

They belonged to a tusker killed by an Indian maharajah.

A majestic crystal chandelier lit up the remains of the departed animals.

The Gorkha Baithak—the large chamber that got its name from the native land of the Shah kings—was in the centre of the building. A huge chandelier with three-layered crystal formations hung in the middle, over the paintings of the eight mother goddesses who are believed to protect the city of Kathmandu from evil and danger. The silver throne of the king and queen was placed on one side, eight feet high and adorned with the nine heads of the mythical sea serpent, the Sheshnag, looming over the backrest.

Chandeliers also glittered in the nearby Tanhu Room, with more regal mementos, including a beautifully carved wooden throne, with a canopy of a life-like mesh of leaves, tree branches and creepers. Next door, King Tribhuvan's room—or Mugu Baithak—preserved with extreme care, was a fascinating display of French glass furniture, down to the hookah, a clock, a waste basket, a lampshade and an array of other designer items. Nearby, a portrait of King Birendra was surrounded by clocks from across the world.

These clocks were ticking away furiously—the Friday night dinner was approaching.

Dipendra was tired. Between the visit to the sports complex and the priest's house, it had been a long day. He went to his chambers, showered and started changing for the evening soirée. Wearing a shirt and trousers, and accompanied by his ADC Gajendra Bohra, he set out for the Billiard Room where the party was scheduled. It was almost 6:45 p.m.

Dipendra was walking in the section called Tribhuvan

Sadan, where both his residence and the party venue were located. He climbed over a small bridge, walked through a garden flanked by pillars and pushed open the door of the large but unostentatious Billiard Room. It was vacant. The British-era snooker table, after which the room was named, was kept at the far end, surrounded by a jute rug for players. The sofas had been neatly arranged for the evening, in two U-shaped formations at opposite ends, and the drinks arranged in the small bar on one side of the room. The whiskeys, for which there would be the most takers, were on the top shelf—Dimple, White Horse, Johnnie Walker, Famous Grouse . . .

Bohra wanted to take leave to go and change as well, but Dipendra stopped him. For a long time, the crown prince pottered around the snooker table, as Bohra passed him the balls. More than forty lazy minutes passed.

Chefs were working away in the din of the royal kitchen, preparing a lavish spread. In the dining hall next to the Billiard Room, kitchen staff laid red utensils and fancy cutlery.

Brooding, the crown prince bent over the snooker table and played several shots, then walked across the half-carpeted hall to pour himself a drink. This was his favourite: Famous Grouse.

It was past 7:15. In contrast to his mood at the priest's house, the outward demeanour of the crown prince was cheerful, effervescent—like on any other day.

In other parts of the city, several cars had driven out of swank villas and were now making their way through the busy Kathmandu roads. The guest list for the dinner was short, with twenty-five people to attend, including the king, and the guests knew they had to be on time.

A grey Nissan Sunny was the first car that drove into the palace, through the Western Gate. The two pillars at the gate had been painted in the likeness of a snow-capped mountain peak. The effect was not convincing; the pillars appeared more like two huge ice-cream bars to visitors. At the wheel was a slim, jovial, elderly man in glasses. Maheshwar Kumar Singh was never embarrassed about being the first guest: for five decades, he had always reached royal gatherings before time.

Singh had been related to Nepal's royal family since 1952. He was then the prince of the Indian state of Sarguja in a thickly forested, mineral-rich region of eastern India. He married Princess Vimala Rajya Lakshmi, daughter of King Tribhuvan and became the royal son-in-law. That would make him the uncle of King Birendra. In 1955, King Tribhuvan died and Singh came to Nepal for the first time to attend the thirteenth day mourning ceremony. The next year, King Mahendra, was enthroned. Singh came for the ceremony and, at the insistence of the then queen mother, stayed on in Nepal.

Singh was wearing the traditional Nepali dress that all citizens had to wear when they went to the palace: a white labada—a long shirt—and the sural, which are tight pyjamas. He also wore a jacket and the traditional Nepali cap.

Soldiers dotted the area along the 150-metre drive from the gate to the Tribhuvan Sadan. Two entire battalions of the Royal Nepalese Army were posted inside the palace, based on the southern and northern sides. One of them, the Purana Gorakh Regiment, had beaten other elite army units in equestrian, athletics, and other sporting events two years ago to win the honour of receiving the King's Banner and protecting his palace. The other, the Kalibahadur Regiment, had been deployed on 1 April.

The palace was first built in 1847 by Jang Bahadur, the first of the Rana clan prime ministers who kept the Shah dynasty kings virtually as prisoners for more than a century and controlled the country. Jang Bahadur wanted to build a residence for his brother, and after a meticulous survey, had opted for an area that was then outside city limits. The chosen plot of land had a spring, and a temple to Lord Vishnu where thousands flocked each year. Construction began. Workers swarming the area with shovel and pickaxes created a broad road where none existed. This was called the Durbar Marg or the King's Way, the broad avenue that led straight to the main Southern Gate of the palace. It was the king's neighbourhood. It was the best address in town.

The Ranas, influenced strongly by Western architecture, marked the stamp of British castles on what came to be known as the Narayanhiti Palace. It took seven years to build. Over the years, the palace was landscaped on an ambitious scale. There were European-style pools, beautiful gardens dotted with statues and a bandstand. The broad marble stairway leading to the palace interiors was draped in a red carpet. The halls inside—like the one where Crown Prince Dipendra used to hold a reception each year on his birthday—were lined with paintings and pictures of past rulers.

But the huge building—splendid but weak—was torn down in 1970, during the reign of King Mahendra, to rebuild the new Narayanhiti Palace, the current home of the Shah kings spread across 40,820 square feet of space. The entire palace compound covers an area of fifteen acres.

There were still silver gilded doors, fancy chandeliers, hundreds of servants and the trappings of royal grandeur, but probably not of the level of the ostentatious Rana kings. Despite the huge business stakes of Prince Gyanendra, the younger brother of King Birendra, Nepal's royal family was not awfully rich. Their main wealth was tradition—and the unquestioned faith and reverence of millions of Nepali people who looked on their monarch as a god.

Maheshwar Singh drove straight down the metalled road, along a tree-lined stretch, then turned left towards the Tribhuvan Sadan. For many people, this part of the palace often brought back haunting stories they had heard from their elders. According to the tales, Rana Udip Singh, the brother of Jang Bahadur and the occupant of the palace, was killed in the same location by his power-hungry nephews.

The apparent cause of the murder was the complex succession procedure decreed by Jang Bahadur: every prime minister would be succeeded one by one by his brothers, and then a similar cycle would run from the eldest nephew onwards. Jang Bahadur had seven brothers and seventeen impatient nephews. The wait for power seemed just too long.

After the murder, Rana Udip Singh's palace was converted into the official residence of Nepal's king. King Tribhuvan would be the first Shah dynasty king to break free from the Rana stranglehold in the 1950s. Since then, the kings had often used the lawns outside the main building to gallop on their white steeds in their spare time, or to practise their skills at the shooting ranges inside the palace compounds. Their princes drove around in fancy motor-driven bicycles around the maze of palace roads. The queens could stroll through the manicured lawns and along the tree-lined paths and chiselled hedges, where one could see water spouts with carved serpent deities.

Despite the serenity, the palace was well fortified. Taxi drivers were afraid to even slow down their vehicles anywhere near the gates of the palace—many had been thrown into prison. Poorly armed but fiercely indoctrinated Maoist guerrillas had begun sweeping across parts of the country in 1996 with their people's revolution, and they seemed to mean serious business. In recent times, the main focus—and fear—of the security phalanx at the royal palace was the possibility of a surprise attack by hordes of Maoists.

A four-layer security cordon ringed Nepal's king. Men from Nepal Prahari, the national police force, formed the outermost layer, standing with truncheons around the palace periphery. The second ring was the armed members of the military police at different gates, guarding the immediate vicinity of the palace. Across the palace compound, several thousand soldiers of the Royal Nepalese Army were deployed. The innermost circle consisted of the ADCs, the best men from Nepal's security forces, trained all over the world to be shadows of the royal family. It was the most secure place in the mountain kingdom.

Or so they thought.

In the Billiard Room, Queen Aiswarya was about to come and the party would then be reduced to a private gathering where the ADCs would not be allowed. Bohra prepared another drink for the crown prince, and walked out of the hall towards his office, fifty metres away. It was 7:25 p.m.

Almost at the same time, Maheshwar Singh's car pulled up in the parking lot outside. Singh walked past the area where the ADC rooms were located, through a small garden full of flowers, and then turned left into a veranda to face the only open entrance to the Billiard Room.

He waited there for almost four minutes, until it was precisely 7:30 p.m., and then was ushered into the hall, where the crown prince was walking about, alone.

Singh bowed and greeted Dipendra. The crown prince smiled back. He stopped playing.

'What will you have to drink?' the crown prince asked. He was tending bar today.

'What's the hurry? Let others come, Your Highness,' Singh replied respectfully.

'No, no, you will only help me if you start now. Later there will be so many people. There'll be a rush,' Dipendra said.

'I'll have a whisky,' Singh said.

'Which one?'

Singh took a quick look at the bar. He was a connoisseur of whiskeys. The choice was instant.

'I'll have Famous Grouse,' he said.

'Oh, great . . . I am also having Famous Grouse,' Dipendra said, as he held up his drink. He then picked up the bottle and slowly poured the drink into the glass. A few cubes of ice. Some water.

For a royal quarter, this part of Tribhuvan Sadan was an awkward construction, partly because portions had been added to it over the years that jutted out and spoilt the symmetry. The largest room was the Billiard Room, with a snooker table brought generations ago from Britain. There were three large windows, all on one side, opening towards the east into the veranda and close to a bathroom. Another, much small rectangular room had been built adjacent to the main chamber, but it had no partition except for a row of sofas, and made the Billiard Room look like an 'L' with a disproportionately fat base. A small bar was located at the corner where these two rooms met. Across the eastern windows, the corridor and the bathroom was another small chamber, called the Sano Baithak, where the queen mother usually rested while parties were on. There was another reason why she remained there, and not in the Billiard Room hubbub: according to protocol, no one could smoke in her presence, not even the king. Except one man—the king's uncle, also a guest that evening.

That gentleman was walking in now: stocky, seventy-six years old, with a freckled face, two large tattooes of Hindu goddesses on his arms and a cute smile on his lips. Like Singh, retired general Rabi Shumshere Rana was also a son-in-law of King Tribhuvan. The wives of Singh and Rana were sisters.

Rana, an artillery officer with the Royal Nepalese Army until 1968, had also frequented the palace for five decades: his niece was the first wife of King Mahendra. He was also an ace officer: Rana was the first ever graduate of the Indian Army's artillery school in Deolali in western India

As he had done for the past four years, Rana was going alone to the palace today. His wife, Princess Tika

Rajya Lakshmi Devi, had died in 1997.

Rana gingerly entered the Billiard Room. The royal ladies also started arriving almost simultaneously: Queen Aiswarya herself, and the king's three sisters—Princesses Shobha, Shanti and Sharda—all went and sat on sofas placed along the same wall as the snooker table, near Princess Helen, King Birendra's aunt. The crown prince was still flitting between the table and the bar. His sister, Princess Shruti, had arrived with her husband, Kumar Gorakh Shumshere Jang Bahadur Rana.

Rana bowed and greeted the ladies with a namaste, who smiled back.

Dipendra had soon served Rana a drink of White Horse whisky. The crown prince was perfectly sober, walking, talking and behaving exactly as he would on any other day. His gait was erect, his walk brisk.

It was now past 7:30 p.m. Cars started driving into the porch. Cousins, uncles, aunts, brothers, sons-in-law, daughters greeted each other as they entered. Cell phones rang. The Billiard Room slowly started buzzing with seemingly endless Friday night banter. Nepal's first family was ready to lazily slip into another weekend.

'Shall we play a game?' Dipendra asked Rana, looking towards the snooker table. Rana, who had played with Dipendra since his childhood, and had accompanied him on numerous hunting trips, clutched his left hand with his right one.

'I'm sorry, but my hand is not moving properly. I had a bad fall at home,' Rana said.

As he took the first sip of his drink, he turned around. Queen Aiswarya, in a red sari, was walking towards him with a packet in her hand.

'I have a present for you. I brought this for you

from China,' the queen said. She had recently returned from a state visit there with King Birendra. 'I know I have delayed giving it to you.'

It was the last gift the queen would give anyone— a packet with a leather belt, a wallet and a pen.

At the other end of the room, behind the bar, Dipendra was talking to Captain Rajiv Raj Shahi, an army doctor. Shahi was also the son-in-law of Dhirendra Shah, the youngest brother of King Birendra. Born a prince, Dhirendra had lost his royal title when he divorced his wife, Princess Prechhya, went to live in England and married a British woman. He later broke up with her too and returned to Prechhya, but never got back his royal title. Princess Prechhya and Princess Komal were both sisters of Queen Aiswarya.

Shahi played snooker for some time and then walked to the farthest end of the room, near the CD player, to sit with the rest of his group.

At about 7:40 p.m., Prince Paras arrived, accompanied by his wife Himani and his mother Princess Komal. Paras was the son of Prince Gyanendra, who was away on work, staying overnight in the mountain resort of Pokhara.

Paras and his wife walked to near the bar, where the young crowd was huddled. In deference to the elders, the youngsters were smoking at a point where they were hidden from the rest of the room. Cigarette cases were flipped open. Some smoked Cartier, others Marlboro or 555.

Nepali music wafted from the CD player. Some young royals tried their hand on a carom board placed nearby.

Dipendra, now with a cocktail in hand, came and

sat on a sofa with Paras, who was drinking Coke.

'I am sitting here with whisky. Why are you having just Coke?' the crown prince said. Paras smiled.

They started chatting. Dipendra seemed distracted and restless.

'What happened? What's wrong?' Paras asked.

'I spoke to Mua (mother) about the marriage . . . I also talked to the Queen Mother. They are both against it. Now I will talk to His Majesty on Sunday.'

Suddenly, he seemed very drunk.

'I think I am a little high,' Dipendra turned around and told Dr Shahi. As his friends and cousins would recount later, this was against his normal behaviour: Dipendra was the most composed drinker at parties, never losing his calm even after more than ten or twelve glasses of whisky, which he loved. He had sometimes sat with friends over drinks until 4 a.m., and then got ready for official functions at eight. But today, he already seemed shaky after a drink or two. 'I have to go now and fetch the queen mother,' he said.

It was a few minutes to 8 p.m.

The crown prince walked up to his mother, who was with Princess Helen Shah in the central part of the room. Dipendra leaned over and muttered to Queen Aiswarya: 'Shall I go and receive the queen mother?' The queen gave her permission.

He walked to his Land Rover and drove to Mahendra Manzil, the royal mansion of the queen mother. Meanwhile others trooped in. The king was delayed— he was in the middle of a seventy-five-minute meeting with magazine editor Madhav Rimal.

In the Billiard Room, the men huddled together, engaging in a polite conversation about the weather.

Then the queen mother arrived in her Mercedes, holding her purse and a hand fan kept in a cotton bag.

The elder guests rushed to pay their respects to her, after she walked straight to the small chamber adjoining the Billiard Room. The queen mother would remain here for most of the evening with Princess Helen Shah.

In another part of the palace, King Birendra was winding up the interview. He rose from his chamber and gave last-minute instructions to Mohan Bahadur Pandey, his press secretary. Pandey then sought the monarch's leave, and saw the king walk away towards the venue of the party. The king's ADC, Gen. Sundar Pratap Rana, walked him to the Tribhuvan Sadan.

In the Billiard Room, Dipendra returned to his drink. Then he flipped out his stylish Motorola mobile phone and made two quick calls. He first dialled a familiar number: 98102-4339.

The telephone belonged to Usha Rana, his future mother-in-law. Devyani picked up the phone. She was hoping to meet the crown prince that evening, at a party at the residence of her affluent friends, the Malla family. The crown prince would come there after the Billiard Room dinner, if it got over early. Dipendra and Devyani spoke for 1 minute and 14 seconds.

The subject of the conversation is not known, but it seems to have agitated him. A few minutes later, he dialled 98102-1509, the number of his aide, Gajendra Bohra. It was 8:19 p.m.

'Get my cigarettes,' he ordered.

Sitting in the ADCs' room, Bohra hung up and looked for a royal orderly. He found him soon. The orderly knew the drill; he had been doing this for a year. Five cigarettes were quickly laced with hashish. He walked to the eastern gate of the Billiard Room and gave them to the doorman, who passed them on.

The elders were all away in the smaller room now, with the queen mother. The crown prince and the youngsters remained in the Billiard Room.

Minutes later, at 8:25 p.m., Dipendra's telephone rang again. The number flashing on the display was a familiar one: 423051, Devyani's private land line. The crown prince did not take the call. The phone was programmed to transfer all unanswered calls to his ADC, and Devyani was on the line next with Bohra.

She was very worried.

According to her, the crown prince sounded slurred when she last spoke to him, and he spoke slowly. Devyani had panicked and called the two ADCs of the crown prince—Gajendra Bohra at his office, close to the Billiard Room, and Raju Karki at his residence.

'He wasn't speaking properly. His voice was slurred. Is he sick? Could you check in his bedroom?' she told Bohra. The ADC said he would.

Meanwhile at the Tribhuvan Sadan Prince Nirajan walked in, clutching a CD, and walked towards the music system.

In the small chamber, the queen mother sat on a sofa as each guest bowed and paid respects. Rabi Shumshere Rana, Maheshwar Singh, Kumar Khadga, Gorakh Shumshere and the other men sat on chairs and sofas. Princess Helen leaned over and chatted with the queen mother about her recent trip to the hugely popular shrine of Tirupati in southern India.

Then the door opened. King Birendra walked in. He had entered the building and gone, like his mother, directly to the smaller chamber. Sundar Pratap Rana, the ADC, had walked up to the chamber and then returned, since the party was a private gathering. Then he walked back to the ADCs' offices.

The people in the Sano Baithak raised a toast to the queen mother. Glasses clinked. The men toasted with whisky, the women with a cola. The queen mother also held a cola.

'Go, fill up your glasses,' the queen mother told Rana and Singh.

Sensing that the king wanted to be left in private, everybody else left the room except his mother, Princess Helen and Queen Aiswarya. He huddled with them in a deep discussion for about twenty minutes. The subject of their talk is not known. Then the king returned to join the rest.

Some drama was about to take place in the Billiard Room. According to Paras and Dr Shahi, Dipendra soon appeared to lose control of himself. He began to stammer and struggled to keep standing. He swayed, lost control, stumbled, and fell.

It was almost 8:30. The king was about to come into the hall after meeting his mother. It would be a deep embarrassment for King Birendra before his immediate family if the crown prince was seen in this state. According to Shahi and Prince Paras, the crown prince fell down and fainted. Soon he seemed to be asleep.

This was very unusual behaviour. Dipendra was described among his friends as a very controlled drinker. He never started shouting, never became too emotional, never abused and never did anything in a drunken state that went against his honour, grace and position.

Most of all, he had never passed out after having

drinks. Tonight, he had either become the great pretender, or was under high levels of stress.

'Your Highness, please don't sleep here. His Majesty is here. It is not proper for you to sleep here,' Paras said loudly as he bent over Dipendra.

He did not respond. Then Dr Shahi and princes Paras and Nirajan lifted the overweight prince, holding his hands and legs.

Dr Shahi held him on his left side, Prince Nirajan the right, and Paras held his feet as the three hauled him up and carried him. Kumar Gorakh walked behind. The men heaved hard as they lugged the crown prince through the garden, towards his bedroom in the mansion.

When they reached his bedroom, they kept him on a mattress on the floor, not the main bed, apparently too tired to lift him higher.

The crown prince's lethal toys—pistols, sub-machineguns and rifles—were placed in a drawer. Cartridge cases were in the next drawer. The crown prince's fetish for arms was well known.

As the men turned around to go, Paras told Nirajan: 'Take the weapons from here.'

'It's all right, let it be. Why bother?' Nirajan said as he shrugged his shoulders. The crown prince seemed to be asleep. They switched off the lights and walked out, back to the party.

After they left, Dipendra got up and made another call to Devyani Rana. It was 8:39 p.m.

According to Devyani, the crown prince said: 'Goodnight, I will call you tomorrow morning.'

Act One had ended.

Soon after, King Birendra walked out after meeting his mother and joined the rest of the guests in the

Billiard Room. He had a glass of Coke in his hands. Almost a half hour passed.

In the silence of his bedchamber, the crown prince was rising from his sprawled position. Sometime after being left in the room, he had taken off his shirt. Ram Krishna K.C., his valet, came in from the kitchen. Dipendra was inside the bathroom, dressed only in his trousers. Ram Krishna heard him retching.

He stepped out and ordered the staff to leave.

Dipendra took off his shirt and trousers and started changing into an unusual party dress. He wore army fatigues: a camouflage vest, trousers and a jacket, a cap, black socks, boots and black gloves.

'Shall we take the emergency bag, Your Highness?' asked Ram Krishna, standing outside the room. The emergency bag contained a weatherproof jacket, chapstick, spray, extra batteries and other equipment sometimes required when Dipendra was travelling.

'No, it's not needed now,' Dipendra snapped.

There was a reason why Dipendra was in the fatigues: he was now transformed from a crown prince to a commander of the army, and all military aides were, by protocol, bound by authority not to defy him in any circumstance.

In the Billiard Room, Rabi Shumshere Rana, who had barely started his drink, walked out to the veranda. Kumar Khadga stood with him. Kumar Khadga always had one question to ask of the former general.

'So, what is the army doing these days? Do you know something new?' Khadga asked. He was hinting about army deployment to fight Maoist guerrillas.

'No, nothing that I know of,' Rana said. Then he walked back into the room, and a voice stopped him. It was the king.

'Rabi! Come here,' King Birendra called out. 'What do you have to say? What is the news?'

Rana searched for words. 'Nothing to add, Your Majesty,' he said, smiling.

At about 9 p.m., King Birendra sent word to his ADC to fetch his cigar.

In the distance, a young man with a paunch had stepped out of his chamber, dressed in battle fatigues, and was now making his way towards the Billiard Room, crossing the bridge.

Maheshwar Kumar Singh stepped closer to the king. It was time for male bonding. The men were standing in a loose U.

'Sorry, my wife could not come, Your Majesty. She has a gout problem,' Singh said. He stood with his back towards the huge wood-and-glass door of the Billiard Room.

'Uhhhh . . . Gout has become our family problem,' King Birendra said as he stood near the edge of the table, his face towards the bar.

'Another problem is cholesterol. My wife also had it,' Rana said. The king's entire family complained of alarmingly high cholesterol levels.

Unnoticed and unheard, a stealthy shadow entered the room and walked briskly to near the snooker table. It was what would seem to many guests as 'the man in black'.

Maheshwar Singh heard someone's footsteps behind him, to his right. The brisk steps went pat-pat-pat as the hard leather boots hit the shiny marbled floor. Singh looked over his shoulder and saw the crown prince walking towards him, at least one assault rifle in his hand.

Although the crown prince did not seem to have a fetish for coming to Friday night parties in battle fatigues, the dress did not immediately register. Singh turned around and carried on with the conversation.

In the centre of the room, some ladies were also staring at the crown prince. They thought it was an attempt by the crown prince to draw some laughter.

Ketaki Chester, the daughter of Princess Helen, whispered to her elder sister Princess Jayanti: 'Isn't he too old to come in a uniform in front of other people?'

'I don't know,' Jayanti mumbled, puzzled.

'Maybe he is carrying the weapons to show them to His Majesty,' said Ketaki.

Next to the snooker table, Rabi Shumshere Rana froze as he raised his head from his drink. He found himself staring into the stony, expressionless face of Dipendra. The crown prince stood only about six inches away from him. Rana, puzzled, anxious and tense all at once, lifted his eyebrows, as if querying: 'What's up? What's all this?'

Dipendra did not react. He looked at the king, his father, with a face that seemed sapped of all emotion. A split second later, his right finger pressed the trigger on his 9 mm., German-made MP5-K automatic sub-machinegun, which he held pointing upwards, close to his waist. Many could barely see the foot-long weapon.

A deafening burst of gunfire followed. One bullet pumped into the ceiling. Some plaster peeled off.

For a second, it seemed the massive burst had made him deaf. The gunfire seemed to have ripped through Singh's right ear. Singh felt as if a dozen iron nails were piercing his ear. Instinctively, he thrust his index finger in his right ear, and shut his eyes in horror.

Then Dipendra went for his target. His father.

For those who watched the sequence of events over the next few minutes, a massive juggernaut of horrific images was being recorded in their numb minds. It was as if two dozen camcorders were rolling at once, and the shaky images would haunt them for the rest of their lives—if they lived beyond those few blood-soaked minutes.

King Birendra stood a few feet away from Rana, to his left, beside the snooker table. In his immediate semi-circle were Maheshwar Kumar Singh, Gorakh Shumshere, Kumar Khadga and Dhirendra Shah. It was past 9 p.m.

Dipendra looked straight at the king and pressed the trigger. With his eyes still squeezed shut, Singh heard the loud, deafening rattle of an automatic weapon.

Singh opened his eyes, imagining the worst possible. But nothing seemed to have changed. The men were still standing in their semi-circular formation. Their drinks were still in their hands. As far as he was concerned, the party was still on.

For several seconds, the guests stood where they were, frozen, waiting for the next move of a rampaging prince. Onlookers thought Dipendra was having a prank at the expense of others, showing off his new weapons, and that he had misfired.

The crown prince turned around and walked out of the room through the only door, towards the garden adjoining the Billiard Room.

About three or four seconds after the gunshot, the stunned men standing closest to the king realized that Dipendra had not misfired. King Birendra had got hit on the right side of his neck, at least three bullets tearing through the skin and landing somewhere across the room. Another burst had torn through his abdomen. He looked towards the crown prince, shocked and dazed. It was what Singh would later describe as a 'strange look'.

A tiny river of blood sprouted from his injuries. As if in slow motion, King Birendra started falling to his right, along the snooker table.

He slumped slowly, staying on his feet for much longer than one would expect.

The men around him snapped out of their blank state.

'Where is the doctor?' Rabi Shumshere called as the men lunged forward. He hurriedly kept his glass of whisky on the snooker table.

The king was falling. Seconds before the gunshot, his ADC had brought his cigar to the office and was waiting to deliver it.

Queen Aiswarya ran from where she was sitting on a sofa, moving aside people with her arms as she reached close to her husband. She screamed in shock. The king's sister, Princess Shanti, too, was staring in disbelief and horror.

'Oh my God! Call the doctor! Call the doctor!' the queen cried as she rushed out of the room, followed by the princess.

Sitting in his office not far from the Billiard Room, Sundar Pratap Rana looked up in the direction of the hall. The aides were watching a daily television show by Santosh Pant, a hugely popular satirist. Dipendra's ADC was punching away on the computer.

The deafening gunshot had shaken the cupboard in the ADCs' office.

'What was that?' Sundar Rana snapped.

Within seconds, this was followed by the queen's shriek. Sundar Rana picked up his mobile phone and started calling the royal doctor, Brig. Gen. Khagendra Bahadur Shrestha. Rana would later claim that he was calling on the land line.

In the neighbouring district of Lalitpur in the Kopundole neighbourhood, the balding, cheerful doctor was relaxing after dinner at his residence. The telephone was working fine. But the doctor said it just wasn't ringing at the time when Sundar Rana said he was calling desperately from the palace.

Surprisingly, it had also not occurred to the ADCs to call the doctor, who had known and travelled with King Birendra since he was crown prince, on his mobile phone.

Meanwhile, Gajendra Bohra left the computer and stepped out of the office. Then he hopped back.

'Sir, I can hear shots,' he told Rana. The king's ADC was apparently still dialling away, trying to reach the doctor. Dr Shrestha's telephone would finally ring at 9:10 p.m., when Sundar Pratap Rana would inform him of the massacre.

On a nearby table, Major Anant Keshar Shima, Queen Aiswarya's ADC, was busy dialling the number of the Military Hospital. That was one number that always seemed impossible to connect.

In the Billiard Room, Dr Shahi was leaning over the CD player to raise the volume of a song. As he heard the gunshots and the shrieks, he dropped his cigarette, and tore across the room. He had taken a few seconds to realize what had happened. Shahi ran to the king and scampered around him, holding him from the back as he lay him down on the carpet.

Then Shahi took off his ash-coloured coat, and started pressing it against the king's neck to staunch the blood.

'Rajiv, also in the stomach,' King Birendra said, pointing to his other wound.

'Please don't worry about that, Your Majesty. It is important to stop the loss of blood,' Shahi replied as he tied the jacket tighter.

The king tried to raise his head and muttered in Nepali: 'Kay gardeko? (What have you done?)' Those would be his last words.

But he was talking to the air. The man to whom he had addressed those words was already outside the hall, and now turning back for the next assault.

For Rabi Shumshere Rana, with his army background, the immediate requirement was clear. 'Ambulance!' he called out. There would be no ambulance. There weren't even ADCs. There wouldn't even be first aid.

In the ADCs' office, Sundar Pratap Rana was busy on his walkie-talkie: 'Immediately send Fighting Force,' referring to a crack commando unit deployed in the palace premises for emergencies.

In a baffling response to Nepal's national emergency, none of the ADCs still had tried to rush to the Billiard Room in time, despite the massive gunshot echo and the queen's shriek. They were sitting at a distance that would have taken them less than ten seconds to scamper across.

In the queen mother's chamber, she and Princess Helen were chatting away when the gunshots were heard.

'There is firing going on,' the princess said, panicking.

'Oh, there he goes shooting cats and crows again,'

the queen mother muttered.

The crown prince's fetish for doing shooting practice inside the palace expanse—targeting bats, cats, crows and other birds—was well known. But according to the king's close aides, whenever Dipendra went on such a shooting spree, the security forces inside the palace were informed well in advance, so there would be no panic.

In the Billiard Room, King Birendra lay motionless and prostrate, his legs spread out in the direction of the bar.

Rana said again, to no one in particular: 'Shall we evacuate him immediately?' No answer.

A stunned silence settled on the room. The King of Nepal was dying on the carpeted floor. When word leaked outside the Narayanhiti Palace, it would seem the end of the world for his country's people. But for now, there was just bewilderment.

No help would come for some time. Instead, the one to come in was the crown prince. He darted in, approximately ten seconds after his first strike.

New attack. New gun.

The crown prince tightly held a 5.56 millimetre, U.S.-made M-16 A2 telescopic rifle as he briskly walked back into the Billiard Room. A green nylon sling hung carelessly from the gun as he walked. Dipendra marched ten feet into the room, looking straight ahead, emotionless. Suddenly someone tried to confront him.

'Baba, enough! You have done enough damage, give me the gun,' Dhirendra Shah ordered as he tried to lunge forward.

This defiance did not go with Dipendra's plan. It was enough to infuriate the proud prince, who eyewitnesses said was now provoked into more ferocity.

Punishment was swift. Within a second, bullets ripped through his uncle's chest. But the king's youngest brother did not die immediately.

There was a moment's pause. Then Dipendra started spraying the room with bullets.

Kumar Gorakh Shumshere Rana, the husband of the king's daughter Shruti, leaped to a side and hid behind a table when a bullet grazed his neck. He fell wounded in a heap. Gorakh would be relatively lucky: he would survive with lacerated lips and neck, and a torn vein. His right thumb, however, would be amputated in hospital.

His wife, was meanwhile running towards her father.

'Bua! Bua!' she cried, addressing him in Nepali. Then she saw that Gorakh had fallen too.

'You too have been hit?' she said. Shruti changed her course towards Gorakh. 'Baba, what happened? What happened?'

She reached her husband and cradled him in her lap, holding him with shaking arms. That attracted her brother's attention—and his bullets. The next burst from Dipendra sheared the left elbow of his sister. She fell over her husband and lay unconscious.

Paras, standing near the bar, yelled hoarsely to his sisters: 'Sit down! Lie down! Hide under the table!'

From the ADCs' room, Sundar Pratap Rana now started running, finally, towards the Billiard Room, followed by some other ADCs. But he wanted to avoid the main entrance because gunshots had been heard from that direction. He headed towards another entrance—a six-foot-wide window-cum-door located behind the snooker table, which was part ornate wooden panel and part movable glass window.

The painted glass shut out the view from inside the room. But along the other wall, facing the veranda, there were three other windows, with clear glass and curtains drawn. The ADCs could have seen what was happening inside the room. Some of them had even seen the crown prince walk away, heavily armed with weapons.

Inside, the crown prince did something any assassin would have considered suicidal in the same circumstances. He threw one of his weapons—the MP5 submachine gun—on the floor.

This was an astounding move. Some would say that he threw it only because its magazine was jammed. Others would see it as a calculated risk on the part of the crown prince. Purely on the basis of intelligent guesswork, some royal cousins would later deduce the following: he had another gun ready, and by throwing the pistol near the victims—some of them with prior military training—he was perhaps tempting them to snatch it and aim it at him.

If anyone did that, it would leave a set of fingerprints that could later help him shift blame. As for his own fingerprints, there weren't any on the guns: he was wearing black leather gloves.

If he had such a plan, it worked, but only just: someone did try to pick up the gun, but it was the wrong man.

It was the king himself.

According to his sister, Shobha Shahi, the king tried to get up and seized the weapon, apparently trying to shoot his son. But Shobha, concerned about Dipendra and confident he would do no further damage, suddenly yanked it from him.

'Leave this,' she snapped.

In the melée, the magazine came off. Shobha threw it away. The last chance to prevent further carnage was lost.

It seems that someone else also tried to use a weapon against the crown prince, but failed: a pistol that had been issued to Prince Nirajan would be found later on the carpet of the Billiard Room along with magazines, Dipendra's MP5 and hundreds of cartridges. This was a 9 mm G19 Glock pistol.

Within moments, Dipendra started firing again from his telescopic rifle, now turning it on Kumar Khadga Bikram Shah, the thickset former lawyer who married the king's sister Princess Sharda. Kumar Khadga fell immediately after being shot through his chest.

Princess Shobha, who had, perhaps unwisely, snatched the weapon from the king moments ago, got in the way of some flying bullets. She ended with the right side of her face and her wrist lacerated.

At the southern end of the room, Dr Shahi had stealthily crept towards a large window, to commit an act unbecoming of a Royal Nepalese Army officer and a doctor: he stole out of the window and ran out of the palace through the Western Gate. He even left his wife Puja and other close relatives trapped inside. Then he did something more surprising—although a fleet of cars, including his own, waited in the Tribhuvan Sadan parking lot, Shahi says he took a taxi to the hospital. He would later claim that he had escaped the hall to summon the ADCs.

Shahi's action would evoke curiosity and suspicion. It would also make one man unemployed: the guard at the Western Gate of the palace who saw Shahi run out

The royal family. From L to R: Crown Prince Dipendra, King Birendra, Prince Nirajan, Queen Aiswarya and Princess Shruti.

King Birendra as a boy.

Crown Prince Birendra with King Mahendra.

King Mahendra with family. Crown Prince Birendra is in the centre behind King Mahendra.

Crown Prince Birendra and Princess Aiswarya at their wedding, February 1970.

King Birendra at his enthronement, 1972.

King Birendra in full regalia.

King Birendra outside
Narayanhiti Palace.

Prince Nirajan, the younger son.

Princess Shruti.

Princess Shruti at her wedding, 1997.

The people's king.

Queen Aiswarya meeting children. The queen was known for her social service.

King Birendra at the opening ceremony of a global initiative for children.

The king and queen at Puri, Orissa.

King Birendra meeting Hillary Rodham Clinton.

and did not stop him was sacked the next day.

In the Billiard Room, Dipendra lifted his gun again and mercilessly pressed the trigger. He aimed at his father, once more, and pumped him with more bullets. This time a bullet penetrated his brain. Bullets were flying all over as the rest of the guests watched in horror, hiding behind sofas, standing helplessly or just waiting for their turn. The barrel turned grey with heat.

King Birendra's blood-stained cap had fallen to a side. His glasses slid off his ashen face.

Meanwhile, Dipendra retreated again towards the door, stepped out, then turned back.

Princess Sharada was rushing towards the king when she saw her husband, the roly-poly Kumar Khadga, sprawled on the floor in a pool of blood.

'You too? What happened to you? What happened to you?' she wept as she ran forward, only to be riddled with bullets at close range. She fell on her husband, her body lying almost diagonally across his. Several bullets had torn into her neck and one side of her face. She died soon.

One bullet ripped through Princess Komal, wife of the king's younger brother, Prince Gyanendra. It pierced below the shoulder, leaving a large wound. The bullet would leave several lacerations on her left lung. She went crashing near a sofa, her glasses flying off, the fall leaving her with multiple fractures in her ribcage. She started gasping for breath.

Someone was knocking at the door.

Gajendra Bohra had run up to the hall and was shaking the door wildly to open it, but says he found it was locked from inside. Amazingly, he turned back towards his office.

Next, Dipendra fired one bullet at close range at Princess Shanti, Sharada's sister, shattering her skull and killing her instantly. Shanti toppled over in a heap, falling on top of Princess Komal.

Princess Komal felt something sticky on her forehead and thought at first she had another wound in the head, then realized that it was spilling from Princess Shanti's injury.

Doctors would save Princess Komal. She would be queen.

Princess Jayanti, the king's cousin, was also on the carpet within seconds, her brain punctured by bullets.

Ketaki Chester toppled over after a bullet punched a deep wound in her right shoulder, tearing flesh and showing up fractured bone pieces.

His eardrum still hurting from the first gunfire burst, the king's uncle, Maheshwar Singh, stood stunned in one corner of the hall—the most unsafe corner.

'You are in the line of fire! Duck! Duck! Duck!' Prince Paras screamed as he saw Singh standing dazed.

The crown prince had darted out again past the glass door and could come back in any moment. Singh ran for his life from near the sofas by the snooker table, towards the sofas at the other end of the room. As he entered the 'U' formation of the sofas, he sprawled on all fours on the floor, lying on his stomach, and brought his arms over his head and folded them. He lay absolutely still, not moving his head or limbs or fingers.

Singh was trying the oldest trick in the book: he was pretending to be dead. It worked.

A few metres away, several women—including Paras's wife Princess Himani—cowered in fear as they hid behind the bar and a CD player, protected from Dipendra's view.

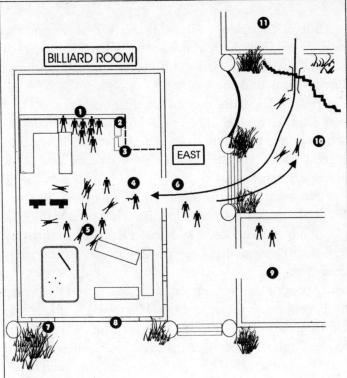

BILLIARD ROOM

EAST

1 Ladies and Paras.
2 CD player.
3 Bar.
4 Crown Prince Dipendra.
5 King Birendra.
6 Main door: Crown Prince came in from here.
7 King evacuated from here.
8 Dr Shahi escapes.
9 Sano Baithak: Queen mother was here.
10 Buddha statue.
11 Dipendra's room.

N

Diagram not to scale

But not for long. Dipendra walked in again, this time coming the farthest inside the Billiard Room, close to the bar, and stood near a chair, aiming his gun at Prince Paras and the women.

He and Dipendra had grown up together, and Paras was said to be the only one who could persuade the crown prince on knotty issues. Paras was also Dipendra's biggest backer on the issue of his marriage. Today, he pleaded for his life.

'No brother, no brother, no brother, no brother,' Paras pleaded in Nepali as he raised his arms helplessly.

'What are you doing? Please! Please go from here,' he said. 'Please, what are you doing, we are the only ones here.'

Dipendra did not immediately go away. He seemed to be enjoying the attention. He stared hard at the women in the corner, examining each face. Expressionless, he craned his neck and leaned forward a few centimetres. The fear of death was painted on each face.

No one knows what made Dipendra change his mind, but he suddenly gestured with his hands, as if saying: 'OK, I let you go'—the only expression of any kind from him during the carnage. Then he turned around and walked out—for the last time—leaving behind a room full of bodies and a carpet soggy with blood.

Paras and several other stunned eyewitnesses were regaining their senses. He tried to take control of the situation. Outside, the king's ADC Rana was roaming around confused and anxious. He was looking for the king in the Sano Baithak, the small chamber where he had left him. Finally he spotted the king, but decided against going in by the main entrance since he feared that the attacker could fire again.

Rana then went out and broke open a window behind the snooker table, shattering a huge pane and sending shards of glass flying. Dozens of soldiers, members of the Fighting Force, also stormed in, wearing combat fatigues. The evacuation began.

'First take Their Majesties! Then those who are injured! Leave the dead for now!' Paras shouted repeatedly to the guards. Then he turned to the casualties and hollered: 'There is no time! Those who are alive should run out!'

Three ADCs rushed towards the snooker table and picked up King Birendra's limp body. They pressed his head with their hands, trying to stop the blood as they evacuated him through the broken window.

Major Shima, the queen's ADC, rushed out to summon all possible cars and other vehicles immediately available. He looked around in the muddle of the bloodied bodies and in the adjoining room—the queen was nowhere in sight. He ran back to the ADC room and dialled the queen's chamber.

The phone kept ringing. Finally a maid picked it up. No, the queen was not there. He headed for the garden.

In the Billiard Room, Prince Paras rushed forward, stopping for a moment by Dhirendra, who could not move his leg. He massaged it for a few seconds. Some metres away, his mother, Princess Komal, was struggling to get up, still holding her head which was smeared with the blood of her sister-in-law.

'I am not OK, I am not OK,' she kept mumbling.

Ketaki Chester pleaded to every passing person for help.

'Rabi Uncle, I have been hit in my shoulder,' she moaned as Rabi Shumshere Rana walked by.

Paras then raced to the small chamber where the queen mother sat.

Unaware of the events, the queen mother was resting with Princess Helen.

'Brother has shot His Majesty the king and so many others,' Prince Paras told her.

'What?' The queen mother leaped from the sofa and tried to run towards the door. Maheshwar Kumar Singh stood dazed outside, his arm bleeding heavily from a bullet wound. The queen mother was stopped and instead Princess Helen rushed into the Billiard Room. The room was a gory switchback to the gut-churning Kot massacre of the royal family in another Kathmandu palace. Helen rushed back.

'Everyone is dead. Except Dhirendra,' she told the queen mother.

'Where is His Majesty?' the king's mother asked.

'I have already sent him to the hospital,' Paras said.

Queen Aiswarya was already following Dipendra towards the garden, perhaps confident that she was the only one who could stop the prince. Prince Nirajan also went after his mother, walking down the inner garden towards the crown prince's quarters.

Ketaki Chester said from where she was lying sprawled on the ground: 'Your Majesty, don't walk out like this . . . don't go there!'

Shortly after, two bursts of gunfire followed. The first hail of bullets ripped through Nirajan's supple body.

Did Dipendra kill his mother and brother too? According to circumstantial evidence, he shot both of them but there was no eyewitness to confirm this.

Nirajan fell on the grass in a pool of blood, much of it gushing from his right ear. Two bullets had ruptured his brain. His right shoulder was shattered. There were at least ten other deep wounds.

From the kitchen, errand boy Santa Kumar Khadka was watching what would turn out to be the last minute of Queen Aiswarya's life.

The queen confronted the crown prince briefly. Both were, according to Khadka, 'shouting and screaming'. The lifelong tussle between the headstrong crown prince and his tough mother had climaxed. It was a bitter moment. Then the queen is believed to have started running towards the crown prince's own residence across the garden, screaming as she ran. Her motive is unclear— perhaps she was seeking shelter, or one of her son's weapons to defend herself. The crown prince started walking backwards. The queen started rushing up the staircase to his bedroom, managing to climb seven steps, when she was shot through the head. Her skull was blown off as the bullets punched into her. She fell on the marbled steps, below a tiger skin hung on the wall.

No one had seen him kill his mother, but according to circumstantial evidence, Queen Aiswarya, shot from behind, had become the last victim of the crown prince's fury.

So merciless was the attack that the body was all but headless. There were more bullet wounds on her body—four entry wounds on the left shoulder alone.

Part of her red sari was torn in the fall and her body was awash in blood that mixed with the bright colours of her clothes and pink socks.

Ketaki Chester's warnings had come true. As she heard the two rounds of firing, she told Prince Dhirendra, also lying wounded nearby: 'The queen is also gone.'

Dipendra walked to the bridge over the pond, where, according to one account, he 'screamed like a mad man once or twice'.

Then the last gunshot rang out.

The survivors shaking inside the Billiard Room heard the boom, followed by complete silence.

Crown Prince Dipendra collapsed on the bridge, falling with a loud thud. He lay on his back, a bullet through his head.

At the same time, his father was being carried out to the front porch, where the king's Jaguar was waiting.

There was no eyewitness to confirm the manner of the crown prince's death. That secret shall probably remain forever within the walls of Tribhuvan Sadan. But there is enough evidence to suggest that there were missing links related to the last minute or so of the crown prince's life.

As the survivors started getting up from among the heaps of the dead, Gajendra Bohra came running in, shouting: 'He shot himself! He shot himself!'

Paras asked Bohra about the fate of the queen and Prince Nirajan.

'Prince Nirajan has been shot. Her Majesty the queen is down. She has no chance,' Bohra said, panting.

Soldiers were now streaming into the room and across the garden, scouring for the dead and the seriously wounded.

As the ADCs and members of the Fighting Force lifted the crown prince, one soldier took a gun from his body—his last weapon—and flung it away. Another

5.56 mm M-16 A-2 rifle was mysteriously found in another lawn nearby, near a statue of the Buddha.

Dipendra's 9 mm pistol, apparently responsible for his death, and empty cartridges were found lying in the pond. It was not certain whether it was the same weapon that the soldier who came upon him flung away.

There was a one centimetre entry wound on the left side, just behind his ear, and a large exit wound on the right side, above the ear. Blood spurted from both. But the crown prince was still alive—he was groaning loudly, apparently having difficulty in breathing.

The worst two minutes in Nepal's modern history had ended. The aftermath was yet to sink in. The booming gunshots of a crazed prince, the gut-wrenching shrieks of terrified victims, the pleading of helpless targets, the soft last words of a dying monarch, the frenzied dying roar of a possessed assassin—all was quiet now.

King Birendra was alive, but just, as the ADCs placed him in the car. Blood oozed out of both his ears. One bullet had gone through his skull, blowing up the top. Blood seeped out of deep wounds in several other parts of his body. In all, the king had been riddled with at least eight bullets.

Within minutes, the Narayanhiti Palace, the pinnacle of Nepal's faith, passion and tradition, had become the Shah dynasty's horrific graveyard. Tribhuvan Sadan was littered with used and live cartridges. Its walls were riddled with bullets. Everything seemed to have been left with marks of blood—the carpet, chairs, slippers, coats, purses, spectacles even the stubs of cigarettes.

The Friday night party was over.

Chapter Five

The Trauma Room

KING BIRENDRA HAD survived the massacre.

Even after bullet wounds to his brain, neck and abdomen, the ADCs carrying the king found he was still clinging tenuously to life as they held him gingerly in their arms.

A little after 9 p.m., a Jaguar and a Toyota were racing on the narrow roads towards the cantonment area.

Inside the Jaguar, two men held the king, his eyes closed and his white dress awash in blood. His pulse was all but gone, but the ADCs still saw a very feeble sign of life: his hand moved a little. ADCs Prafulla Bikram Shah and Pawan Khatri had a centuries-old heritage—a Shah dynasty king—in their arms.

The Toyota, following close behind, had the body of Queen Aiswarya Rajya Lakshmi Devi Shah. Her body was in such a state that nine people had to help to place her in the royal escort car.

'Airway! Airway!' shouted the man at the wheel of the Jaguar—the seniormost ADC, Sundar Pratap Rana. The officers knew the standard drill that emergency paramedics around the world call ABC—the initials that remind doctors to check the airway, bleeding and circulation.

The officers opened the mouth of the king, regularly checking to see that nothing was obstructing his breathing. Among many victims in similar situations, a tongue blocking the airway of an unconscious accident victim can be more life threatening than a gaping wound. They lightly placed their fingers in front of King Birendra's nostrils to feel if he was breathing. They checked his heartbeat. They tried to block his wounds and stop the bleeding.

But other things were going wrong. According to Sundar Pratap Rana, a slow truck was blocking the road on part of the road up to the hospital. Amazingly, the ADC said mobile phones had also stopped working.

Dozens of other cars would be trampling the same road and racing up the same hill very soon. The first of those was already on its way. Dr Khagendra Bahadur Shrestha, the jovial royal physician, had known King Birendra since his teens, when he was just a crown prince. Today his life was at stake. Dr Shrestha had dressed up in a jiffy after he put down the receiver at 9:10 p.m., when he got the first information about the shoot-out from the ADCs.

As the car made its roughshod journey up the hill, a hundred thoughts raced through Dr Shrestha's mind. A thousand memories lashed him. His fears, his prayers, his hopes—all were suddenly coming alive.

He was unaware that a few kilometres ahead on the same road, King Birendra had now passed away. Nepal's most loved monarch had died as serenely and calmly as he had lived.

At the Birendra Military Hospital, their destination

a few kilometres away, the phone had been busy for a long time as palace staff repeatedly tried to call and alert doctors about the arrival of the victims. Finally, they found one line free. A dazed ADC was on the line. The operator transferred the call to soldiers behind a large table at the reception, who transferred it to a woman officer.

Lt. Sadikshya Singh was the doctor in charge that night in the large trauma hall. It had been a slow evening. And yet, tonight was one night that Lt. Singh had not been prepared for in her training by her tough army instructors. Until her seniors came, she had to try and do whatever she could to save the victims of the firing. The toughest assignment of her life was about to begin.

She got a bed ready in the trauma hall. The man after whom the hospital was named would soon arrive in its campus.

Within minutes, the Jaguar stopped at the gates. A stretcher was ready. The car with the queen followed.

It was 9:15 p.m.

The ADCs gently took out the king's body and it was carried inside. As soldiers watched, Sundar Pratap Rana brought him inside the trauma hall and placed his body on the first examination trolley—a stretcher on wheels. Nurses rushed to inform Lt. Singh.

The doctor did a quick survey. Blood was still streaming out from both of his ears. King Birendra's right arm and the entire dress were drenched in blood. He showed no signs of life, and no miracle was in sight.

In a clockwork drill, bandage rolls were passed across trained hospital hands and cotton wads pressed on wounds to stop the blood. Singh started cardiopulmonary resuscitation to try and revive the king. Dr Khagendra Bahadur Shrestha was there in minutes.

Dr Shrestha stood by the king's side and did another quick examination of all the vital signs. Then he looked up.

'No hope,' he told the ADC.

On a hospital document titled 'Treatment Book', Dr Singh wrote 'No. 1' as the bed number, and the name of the patient: 'His Majesty the King.'

Then, in a nervous scrawl, she started writing details about the wounds on the king's body.

They filled up a whole page.

Civilian specialists were informed and summoned by the royal staff. Soon an army of Nepal's best neurosurgeons, plastic surgeons, trauma specialists, heart specialists, radiologists and anaesthetists were hurriedly getting ready in their homes after being pulled away from dinner or late night banter.

Meanwhile, the queen had been declared dead on arrival.

Hopes were also lost at the king's side, but efforts continued. He would later be declared brought dead too. Syringes were poked gently into his skin and intravenous drip pumped into both his arms. From an oxygen cylinder, a long tube travelled up the bed into his nostrils, trying to breathe life into him.

The queen mother took charge, giving frequent directions. Top army doctors trooped in now, all examining the king. Everything failed.

Dozens of pairs of headlights were now making their way up the hill, blaring horns. Word had reached the relatives of the victims. They milled around the main gate of the hospital, trying to keep their kin in

Nepal and abroad informed on mobile phones. Royal family members drove right in. Some walked up to the royal vehicles, parked on a side, in which the bodies had been brought in. Curiosity turned quickly to horror when they saw the blood.

A green Toyota Land Cruiser was racing down the same roads and up the same hill. Prince Paras sat in the front seat, next to the driver. In the rear seats, Dipendra's ADCs Gajendra Bohra and Raju Karki held on to Prince Nirajan and the crown prince.

At the hospital, Princess Shruti was brought in another car and placed on a trolley. Her husband followed soon after, walking in with support. It was togetherness in bizarre circumstances: she had fallen on top of him when they fell to the bullets. Now, at the hospital, they lay on beds next to each other.

As resuscitation efforts continued on the king, Dr Singh came to examine Gorakh, who bled from his neck and twiddled his profusely bleeding thumb.

'It's gone,' he declared. It would soon be amputated.

'It hurts a lot in my chest, doctor,' he moaned.

Dr Singh prescribed for him dressing on his thumb, an intravenous drip, oxygen supply and an injection to soothe his nerves.

Princess Shruti lay pale on the next bed. The doctor looked for her pulse. It was difficult to find and barely felt. Shruti was not responding to external sensations. She did not even twitch her pupils when the doctor dazzled her eyes with strong lights. Dr Singh ordered her staff to inject adrenaline.

Dhirendra Shah moaned and complained that he could not breathe. A gold chain that had tightened around his neck was choking him. Maheshwar Singh, with a bullet wound in his elbow, loosened it.

'It's very hot here. Why is it so hot here?' Dhirendra Shah complained.

On another bed, Princess Jayanti's lifeless eyes stared blankly at the ceiling. She was no more.

More cars had followed in an unruly caravan. The other injured and dead were brought up the winding route in different vehicles—Army Gypsies, Tata trailers, a minibus, vans and royal cars.

At approximately 9:30 p.m., Dipendra and his younger brother arrived.

Minutes after the stretcher was carried in, Prince Nirajan was declared brought dead.

Crown Prince Dipendra had killed so many of his family members that night, that the trauma hall was crammed, and all the beds occupied, when he was brought into the hall on a stretcher. So he was placed on the floor, surrounded by his dead or dying kin.

Many others were brought dead: the king's sisters princesses Shanti and Sharada, his cousin Princess Jayanti and Princess Sharada's husband Kumar Khadga Bikram Shah. Those seriously wounded were Prince Gyanendra's wife Princess Komal, Princess Shobha, the king's third sister, Princess Shruti's husband Kumar Gorakh Shumshere and Ketaki Chester, Princess Helen's daughter.

Things looked bleak for Dipendra himself. There was blood spilling out of both sides of his head—from the tiny entry wound on his left temple and the large exit wound on his right temple. His breathing was still very noisy, each breath coming with a gurgling sound. The blood pressure was low, but not alarming at 100/ 60, but his pupils were not responding to light.

Doctors checked his airway and lifted his head to

place it in a higher position. The breathing eased. Dozens of assistants swung into action with the same drill: intravenous fluids, oxygen cylinders, wound dressings. Within minutes, Dipendra was being wheeled to the operation theatre. Army doctors asked the ADCs to call from his residence the man known as Nepal's best neurosurgeon: Dr Upendra Devkota.

Doctors were working the hardest on Dipendra, because they saw him as the patient with the best chances of survival. At the same time, the experts knew the harsh truth they could not tell anybody: there was just a fraction of a chance, and even if he did survive, he would be just a vegetable for the rest of his life.

Regardless of this reality, they tried their best. More dressing was applied on Dipendra's wounds on the operation table. Blood samples were readied. Dipendra's blood group was B+, the same as that of his mother. King Birendra and Princess Shruti were both AB+, and Prince Nirajan had A+.

In a coffee break, the doctors huddled around a table and discussed the next big question: post-mortems. No one was sure what the law said on this. No one could remember right away a constitutional provision barring doctors from performing a post-mortem examination on a dead king. But no one wanted to stick his neck out. The issue was debated threadbare.

'The incident happened in the palace. Maybe the Constitution will not work inside the palace premises,' one doctor said.

No conclusion was reached. Finally, they gave up.

It was not clear, however, why the patients other than the king, about whom the constitutional position was not in doubt, were not sent for post-mortems. In the early hours of the morning, Dr Shrestha ordered his assistants to compile a detailed list of all the injuries to the victims. That would be the closest the patients came to the examination.

Dr Shrestha looked at the crown prince in the operation theatre, and on a hunch, asked his assistants: 'Do you smell alcohol?'

The doctors smelled him from close. He wasn't reeking of liquor. The doctors concluded that the crown prince had not had an abnormally high quantity of liquor—once again casting a shadow on his apparent state of high intoxication in the Billiard Room. There was, however, no test done for drugs or alcohol.

If an ordinary patient wounded like Dipendra had been wheeled into the operation theatre on a normal day, doctors would perhaps have followed a different procedure, following the drill of waiting and observing the patient for 24 hours before taking any step.

There was no way they could follow that procedure now. The man on the operation table before them was the crown prince. There were just too many sensitivities and intricacies involved. The doctors could not take the risk.

The doctors scurrying around anxiously, trying to decide the next step, had to think not only of their medical handbook; they had to keep another book in mind: Nepal's Constitution.

They were in the middle of an extraordinary situation. Nepal's king was dead, but it could not be said officially: according to the Constitution, the throne of the kingdom could not be vacant even for a minute, and a new king had to be named before the old king was declared dead.

The one who was the next in line after King

Birendra was lying in front of them. He was in no position to function as king, even if he survived. He seemed clinically dead, but he could not be declared dead, unless an occupant of the throne was in place. What was to be done next: was there a third alternative?

There was.

The third alternative was currently in the mountain resort of Pokhara. Prince Gyanendra had flown there from the southern forest area of Chitwan hours ago at 3 p.m. He had got the word. His son, Paras, had made the first call to his father after the massacre.

Doctors swarmed the hospital. At the reception, the telephone operator worked the switchboard rapidly, reading from a list of numbers of people across the city. They needed experts. They needed blood donors.

Princess Shobha was also wheeled into an operation theatre. Princess Komal and Dhirendra had tubes jabbed into their chests as army doctors sewed up their wounds with sutures.

In another part of the city, the crown prince's Land Cruiser was speeding down the roads with a royal ADC at the wheel. Not many took note because Dipendra often drove in similar, rash fashion. He rammed into two cars on a street near the Bagmati River. The car soon pulled into Norvic Hospital, one of the capital's main medical centres, and the ADC rushed to the room of Dr Upendra Devkota, the neurosurgeon.

Dr Devkota had just completed one more operation— a neck surgery—and was seated in his chamber discussing the case with the patient's family. Suddenly, a man barged in and asked the relative to go out. The man was an assistant doctor, and he had a big enough reason to justify his behaviour. The assistant did not know much, except that Crown Prince Dipendra had been injured by a bullet. That in itself was a catastrophe for the unsuspecting Dr Devkota. He was soon going to get a series of shocks.

A second later, the royal aide rushed into the doctor's room.

'We have to go to the Military Hospital. The crown prince has bullet injuries,' the ADC hurriedly told the doctor, who was ready to leave. This time, the officer drove even faster and crazier. The doctor sensed deep trouble. He also feared he himself might soon be getting a head injury—the kind he specialized in treating.

All that Dr Devkota, forty-six, had been told was that the crown prince had an injury. But the fact that he was summoned meant that the injury was in the head. The doctor, trained in Glasgow and London at top research centres, was soon going to need all his medical expertise.

Everyone was craving for Dr Devkota's attention when he reached the hospital.

'Over here, doctor,' one voice said. Dr Devkota looked at one bed.

'That way doctor . . . upstairs,' another voice said.

He walked into the trauma hall, and a senior doctor gave him a briefing about the condition of the victims. On the first bed was a grey-haired man he could not identify. He wore a necklace with the picture of Sai Baba on the pendant. Dr Sadikshya Singh was furiously trying to revive the patient, pumping air into his lungs.

Dr Devkota examined the eyes, then reached for the arm to check his pulse.

'He's gone,' Dr Devkota said. He would know only

several minutes later that he was looking at King Birendra.

'It's a disaster. Everybody has been massacred,' Dr Shrestha told the neurosurgeon as they walked a few metres away.

Then they walked from bed to bed, the military doctor unveiling the royals' faces—whatever remained of them.

There was one stretcher on the floor on which a person was completely covered with a sheet. Shrestha pulled it, revealing the bullet-riddled face of Queen Aiswarya—or whatever remained of it. He knelt down, stretched his arms and tried to take her head in his lap.

The first hopeful sight that Dr Devkota saw was the lone woman there who was alive and being resuscitated: Princess Shruti. Despite no serious external injuries, she had a feeble heartbeat and pulse.

Surprisingly, no doctor did a thorough physical examination of Princess Shruti to look for injuries, taking only a cursory look in deference because she was a woman, and because doctors thought she was in shock. This happened although the doctor on duty was herself a woman, and several other female patients in the same ward were also physically examined.

Princess Shruti would hold out only a little more. She died at 9:55 p.m. of internal bleeding in the abdomen.

Dr Devkota, unaware of the chain of events, asked himself who might have been behind the massacre. The military? The Maoists? Minutes later, he was changing into surgical greens and rushing into the operation theatre, past more stretchers of wounded people. He finally had a patient at hand whom he could try to save: the man who had wielded the gun.

Doctors had taken off his bloodstained army fatigues. The doctor made a quick assessment as other specialists watched expectantly. The crown prince's blood pressure and heart rate were fairly all right at 110/70 and 80. He was trying to breathe with difficulty. A tube had been thrust into his throat. Another smaller one was pumping fluid intravenously into his body.

Dr Devkota assessed his Glasgow Coma Score at 4, on which the best score is 15, or normal, and the worst is 3, or vegetative.

The patient was put on a ventilator. He was heavily sedated, and nursing assistants hurried off to get four units of blood, needed for the surgery.

Dr Devkota rushed to the nearest phone. He had to call his wife.

'Something really, really terrible has happened,' he muttered on the phone. 'Almost everybody in the royal family is dead. Lock the doors. Don't let anybody in.'

As the catastrophe unfolded, palace officials were summoned back to work. They drove into their offices late in the night, coming in through the same Western Gate that had been the gateway to so much tragedy earlier in the night. The military police was put on standby. The army was alerted. Doctors worked like clockwork. Dazed and often weeping citizens were on the telephone with their relatives, friends, and palace contacts—anyone who was in a position to know what had happened. Thousands across the world were beginning to log on to the internet as news appeared in trickles on websites.

However, one man was still sleeping peacefully in his home in the Baluwatar neighbourhood.

It was the country's prime minister.

More than two hours after the massacre, Girija Prasad Koirala had not been informed of the worst crisis in Nepal's modern history, unfolding five kilometres from his residence.

The telephone finally rang at the exchange at the main gate of his official residence at 11:10 p.m. A bleary-eyed operator transferred it to Koirala's secretary, who transferred it to the prime minister's bedroom. It was still not a palace official. It was Dr Keshar Jung Rayamajhi, chairman of the Raj Parishad or royal privy council, the powerful body that named Nepal's kings.

Rayamajhi gave him a quick rundown of the events. In seconds, Koirala was fully awake.

'I am going to the hospital, you come there directly,' Rayamajhi said.

Rayamajhi had got a call at 9:45 p.m., about half an hour after the king was declared dead, and an official asked him to 'stand by', giving no further details. Rayamajhi got dressed in his labada and sural and had waited since for the phone to ring, a thousand dark fears crossing his mind. But none of them matched this.

As Koirala hung up, the phone rang again. This time, it was from the palace, from Pashupati Maharjan, the soft-spoken chief secretary, one of the most powerful bureaucrats in the country.

'I am coming immediately, sir,' Maharjan said.

He arrived soon after in the meeting hall on the ground floor. Both sat in Koirala's official car, a bullet-proof black Mercedes. They drove out of the residence as soldiers and policemen watched silently.

They went to the palace first but there were few officials there to brief them. Then they drove to the hospital.

Rayamajhi, the royal council chief, was already there.

'Where is Prince Gyanendra?' Koirala asked the army chief, Prajjwal Shumshere Rana.

'He is in Pokhara, sir. We have sent a helicopter to bring him here,' the army chief said. But it was raining in Pokhara, and the helicopter could not land. The prince started driving towards Kathmandu, accompanied by police escort.

The chief justice, Keshav Prasad Upadhaya, and Parliament Speaker Taranath Ranabhat, huddled in close discussion. As Rayamajhi walked past the beds, looking at the horrific sights on each trolley, he broke down and wept.

Rayamajhi pulled himself together. He was set to have a role in history. He would name two new kings.

'Do we have the death certificates yet?' he asked Dr Shrestha, the main doctor. But Rayamajhi was now stepping into delicate waters. The crown prince was his father's successor, but he was also his father's assassin. Once King Birendra's death was announced, could he be named Nepal's king? Rayamajhi's 125-member council would meet the next morning to deal with the unprecedented situation. He ordered a meeting of the committee after the arrival of Prince Gyanendra.

But first, he needed to know if the crown prince would make it to the morning.

'He is still alive. His heart is beating. His pulse is beating. He is on a ventilator,' Dr Shrestha told Rayamajhi.

'What does that imply?' Rayamajhi asked.

'Mentally and physically, he is unfit,' the doctor said.

As the night wore on, Rayamajhi realized that his council would have few choices: if Dipendra was alive by the next morning he would have to be declared king. And until then King Birendra would not be officially declared dead.

Dr Devkota was in two minds on whether Dipendra should be transferred to the Bir Hospital, located in the valley very close to the palace, where he thought the facilities were better. Finally he realized that the patient would lose his little chances of survival if he was taken all the way back.

Many doctors would question later the need to waste crucial evacuation time in bringing the king and the other wounded to the military hospital, rather than taking them to the nearby hospital with state-of-the-art facilities. That decision might have given doctors a better chance to save the lives of some victims fence-sitting between life and death.

Antibiotics were injected into Dipendra's body. His head was elevated to help him breathe better. A quick x-ray was done. There were no metal particles inside the brain. Assisted by a top plastic surgeon, Dr Devkota and his team of doctors now started enlarging the wound cautiously, their nimble fingers working like master artisans on the most precious head that remained after the massacre.

The doctors were working on a process called 'debridement'. Dead tissue slid out. It was removed. Bone fragments were removed. The wounds were stitched. Then the plastic surgeon got to work, trying to give a skin layer. In effect, they had just cleaned the wound and ensured that no further damage or infection was caused to it from the particles present inside. They could do nothing else.

The crown prince already had the best doctors on his side. Now he needed God. That was all Dipendra Bir Bikram Shah required that night to be able to live: a miracle.

After hours in the operation theatre, Dr Devkota took a coffee break. That was the first time he was told that the man he had been trying to bring back to life was the one who had caused this macabre drama.

An outside attack on the palace—like a swoop by the Maoists—would have been more devastating, he told himself.

Dawn was about to break. At a nearby military helipad, a helicopter was also set to land, carrying a grave-faced man who had journeyed through the night to reach the hospital. After driving for several hours, he had boarded a helicopter at the nearest place where it could land—at Gajuri, 85 kilometres to the west.

At about 5:45 a.m., Prince Gyanendra walked into the hospital, the closest royal family member surviving and the last one to reach. His face was heavy with distress as he looked at the dead. Then he walked up to the hospital library and summoned Dr Shrestha and Dr Devkota. They closed the door behind them.

'Tell me, how is the crown prince?' Prince Gyanendra asked Dr Devkota.

The doctor was matter of fact. Such injuries were normally fatal, he told the prince. Dipendra was alive but the chances were very, very bleak, he said.

The doctors now had to assess if Dipendra was

brain dead. This involved a complex procedure, including several mandatory tests, which would then be verified by two expert doctors. Doctors then ordinarily inform the family members of the choices before the patient: whether to put him on a ventilator and give him life artificially, or to let nature take its course—a euphemism for letting the patient die.

Dr Shrestha put the same question to Prince Gyanendra. His response was matter-of-fact.

'Do all the tests, tell us whether he is brain dead or not, then we will consult the elders and tell you,' he said. The doctors returned to the operation theatre.

His pupils were dilated. That was not a good sign. But when he was pinched hard in the thigh and other parts of the body, he gently twisted his arms and legs. Then he coughed. Dipendra was responding to the stimulus of pain. He was still not brain dead.

That seemed to have settled the constitutional position for the moment. The king's successor was—in a very technical sense—alive.

The gentle, early morning sunlight started to caress the mountains cradling the Kathmandu Valley, lighting up the entire region.

But Nepal's darkest hour had just begun.

Chapter Six

Eleven Questions

ALONG WITH THE debris left by the carnage was also a series of questions that lay scattered across Tribhuvan Sadan a few minutes past 9 p.m.

There were no eyewitnesses who saw the Crown Prince in the last few moments of his conscious life. The official inquiry did not reach a conclusion on what happened in the garden, but its version left readers at the doorstep of the theory that the crown prince shot himself.

However, circumstantial evidence cited before the panel and details emerging in separate interviews raised a strong suspicion: someone else might have fatally shot Dipendra from close range.

There was, however, no concrete proof to back either version.

The royal ADCs—crack commandos, trained across the world in the best military training centres—reacted to the tragedy in a baffling, and sometimes bizarre, manner, bringing their role too under a shadow. Apart from the public inquiry into the massacre, Gen. Shanta Kumar Malla, a famous retired army officer considered very close to the slain crown prince, conducted a secret inquiry for the palace into the apparent security lapses. On the basis of the conclusions of the inquiry, four ADCs were sacked and security strengthened inside the Narayanhiti Palace. Gen. Malla's report was not made public.

One of the most obvious puzzles, and one that used to be the favourite of every detective worth his salt in mystery books, was the curious location of the one-centimetre entry wound that killed Crown Prince Dipendra. It was located on the left side of his head, behind his ear. But the crown prince was right-handed.

Would he strike a complex acrobatic posture, taking his right arm around his head, then behind his ear, to kill himself? If he managed to do so, he would also have to shoot at an angle which made the bullet emerge from the right temple. His close friends and eyewitnesses say he primarily used his right hand. Even if he was ambidextrous, it is surprising that he would shoot himself behind the ear, and not in the forehead. Both his hands were free when he is said to have killed himself: why did he not use his preferred hand, the right one? If a person is killing himself, would he choose the easy way of shooting himself in the temple, or forehead, rather than strain his arm at a difficult angle and take it behind his ear?

According to the testimony of Major Bishnu Khadga before the inquiry commission, a Fighting Force soldier helping take the crown prince's wounded body to the hospital took a weapon from his body and flung it away, saying there was no use for the weapon now.

Which is this weapon? Is it the pistol found in the pond a few metres away, and sought to be described later as the weapon used to commit suicide? If it is, there is no way the crown prince could have had on his body the same weapon he is believed to have killed himself with. Also, why is a soldier who is rescuing Nepal's crown prince—at a time when each second is crucial—bothering to fling a weapon far away? The behaviour is curious and surprising.

The ADCs are huddled around a television set in their office, forty metres away from the Billiard Room, watching a popular political satire. At approximately 9 p.m., they hear the first powerful rattle of automatic weapon fire. It is so powerful that it shakes a cupboard in the room. Seconds later, they hear the desperate shriek of a woman: 'O my God! Call the doctor!'

Let us consider this: Nepal's king, queen, crown prince and the entire top layer of the royal family is gathered inside the room from where gunshots are heard and the queen's shriek is telling the guards that something terrible has happened. ADCs are expected to lay down their lives to save the lives of the royal family members they protect. So, what does the trusted veteran, Col. Sundar Pratap Rana, King Birendra's ADC, and the most senior officer there, do in the next second? Does he run out, load his weapons, ask the other ADCs to spread out around the building, peep in, and try to overpower or start firing at the attacker?

No. He picks up the phone!

Here's the next mystery. Although this immediate response was questionable, Col. Rana claims that he desperately tried to call the royal doctor as soon as he heard the gunshot. The colonel says he used his mobile phone to repeatedly call Dr Khagendra Bahadur Shrestha.

But the phone was not ringing at Dr Shrestha's residence! So why did the ADC give an apparently misleading version of events?

Dr Shrestha was at home, relaxing after having his dinner at his residence in the Kopundole neighbourhood in the Lalitpur district adjoining Kathmandu. His telephone was working. But at the time when Rana claims he was calling him repeatedly, the doctor's telephone was silent. The phone finally rang at 9:10 p.m. at Dr Shrestha's home. It was a call on the land line. Ten minutes later, the doctor was at the Military Hospital, the first senior doctor to arrive.

The royal doctor also keeps a mobile phone. When the chief ADC claims he tried but could not reach the doctor on the land line, why did he not call on the cell phone?

According to Col. Rana, the king's chief ADC, King Birendra 'had survived the attack', as was apparent from the paramedics' survey of his airway, bleeding and circulation.

The journey in the king's Jaguar from the palace to the military hospital took more than twelve minutes, according to the hospital records, which say he was brought dead at 9:15 p.m. King Birendra, therefore, died in the car during the journey to the hospital.

Racing at breakneck speed, the car carrying Dr Upendra Devkota, Nepal's top neurosurgeon, covered a similar distance and reached the hospital in four minutes. That is one-third of the time taken by the Jaguar. According to the top ADC, the car was also a little delayed—amazingly—by a truck going uphill.

Could the king who died in the car shortly before reaching the hospital, have survived if the rescue mission had been more prompt?

Col. Rana adds one more puzzle: he says all mobile

phones in the Jaguar stopped working when the king was being carried to the hospital.

The journey to the military hospital took twelve minutes, but the Bir Hospital, Kathmandu's top medical institution, is next door to the palace. Since the king was alive for some time after the shoot-out, could he have been saved if the rescuers had broken protocol in the emergency and taken the casualties there—rather than the Military Hospital, the designated royal hospital?

Could Princess Shruti have survived the attack? She was the patient with almost no external injuries, but she died at 9:55 p.m., apparently after receiving little care. According to senior military doctors at the hospital, a thorough physical examination of Princess Shruti was not done out of deference because she was a woman! This happened although the doctor on duty that night was also a woman—Dr Sadikshya Singh. Surprisingly, the same deference was not applied in the case of several other women patients.

Major Gajendra Bohra, the ADC to the crown prince, was also in the office, working on a computer, when the first gunshots rang out. He stepped out and told the king's ADC, Col. Rana, that shots were being fired. Bohra is quoted as saying in his testimony before the inquiry commission, in a translation by Nepal's leading weekly newspaper, *Nepali Times*:

'I went straight ahead and reached the broken door. From there my eyes went to the entrance door. I saw the crown prince step out and pulled at the door (broken one). I knew the door would be locked from the inside; then I ran around and peeped but I could not see anything; then I turned back. At that time I saw another ADC coming and moved forward—slowly—because I had seen firearms.'

This sequence of events, which narrates Bohra's version of the moments before Dipendra's death, raises several doubts and questions.

If Bohra's testimony is correct, witness the reaction of the crown prince's ADC—an elite officer, among the best chosen from the army, who has received tough training across the world. Bohra says he was among the first to reach the Billiard Room after the ADCs heard the gunshots. He is armed, and is well aware of the layout of the Billiard Room. What does he do? Does he risk his life, smash the glass, and storm in? Since he does not know who the attacker is, does he run around the hall to protect the crown prince, whom he has seen, curiously, armed and in battle fatigues?

No. He tries to rattle and pull open the door. When it does not open, he returns!

Bohra says that he walked to a 'broken door' when he reached the Billiard Room. The door could not have been broken when Bohra says he reached there—soon after hearing the gunshots. According to the king's ADC, Col. Sundar Pratap Rana, and other eyewitnesses, soldiers kicked at the door and smashed the glass only when they were evacuating the king to safety, moments before the last gunshot was heard. If the crown prince's ADC actually reached the Billiard Room only when the door was broken, he reached there much after he claims he did. What was happening in the intervening minutes?

According to eyewitness Maheshwar Kumar Singh— a royal family relative and the Friday night survivor with the sharpest eye for detail—the door is made of two panels, one half fixed and made of wood, the other opening out and made of painted fuzzy glass. He describes this door as a 'door-cum-window', through which one cannot peep inside if it is closed. If Bohra could see the armed crown prince from there, as he claims (this door is located in the wall facing the main entrance), the door was certainly broken. If Bohra's testimony and the translation are accurate, it only confirms that the ADC reached the site much after he claims—in the final moments of the carnage. Where were most of the ADCs between the first gunshot and until just before the last one?

Bohra says: 'I ran around and peeped but I could not see anything.' This cannot be true. According to Maheshwar Singh, there were at least three Billiard Room windows along the broad corridor, facing the queen mother's room, which were of plain glass, with the curtains drawn. It was from here that Singh had seen the crown prince alone in the room when he was the first guest to arrive. These windows were not in the direct line of fire. If an ADC tried to creep up to them, he could clearly see what was happening inside, and where the danger was from.

Bohra says he saw the crown prince through the broken door—armed and in battle fatigues. He also heard the gunshots and the scream of the queen, asking for medical help. Simple logic—a crack commando's best friend in a crisis like this—would have shown that the only man around with weapons would be linked to the gunshots, which provoked the desperate cry for help. Why didn't he try to stop the crown prince? If he thought that the attacker was someone else, why didn't he rush to save the life of the crown prince?

There is a gap of ten minutes between the time when the first gunshot rang, and the time when the royal doctor was actually summoned. Ten minutes is as good as a lifetime for a wounded king and his family, some of whom could, perhaps, have been saved. Doctors say the first few minutes are the most crucial, and adequate first aid during this time is often crucial in raising the possibility of saving lives. According to eyewitnesses, the massacre was over in approximately two minutes, or a maximum of two and a half minutes. What was happening around the Billiard Room after the massacre in the unaccounted for seven minutes?

Why is Col. Sundar Pratap Rana, the king's chief ADC, cagey on details about the reaction time? When asked by the inquiry commission, why does he say he 'does not remember' the time the operation took from the time of the first gunshot to the time of rescue? Even the traumatized eyewitnesses remember the time duration more accurately than the ADCs.

According to records of the telephone company, calls were made from the mobile phone of the crown prince to the mobile phone of Gajendra Bohra, his ADC, even when Dipendra was on a ventilator, and after he was dead. These calls were made on June 3, 4 and 6. The crown prince was carrying his mobile phone in the party, from where he spoke to Devyani Rana. The phone went with Dipendra to his room when he was carried, apparently intoxicated, by Prince Paras, Prince Nirajan and Dr Rajiv Shahi. It was presumably left in his room when he came to the Billiard Room dressed in fatigues, since rescuers or eyewitnesses have made no mention of the phone on his body.

The answer could be innocuous, or intriguing, but it raises strong curiosity: Who went to the room of the crown prince during his hospital stay and after his death, and called ADC Bohra from his phone?

And the last question:

Why were no post-mortem examinations done on any of the dead?

Chapter Seven

Piecing the Jigsaw

'Yes I am a god now, but the main thing is always what you feel inside, not what people say about you. It is up to all of us to prove that we are special.'

—Crown Prince Dipendra Bir Bikram Shah, 1989

WHY DID THE crown prince carry out the Friday night massacre?

Perhaps we will never know. Perhaps we all know.

The carnage by Dipendra in the Narayanhiti Palace was gruesome and unforgivable. However, as bizarre, macabre and unexplainable the series of assassinations may sound, they seem to be the last piece of a complex jigsaw that can be pieced together by peeping into the crown prince's mind and his life.

He was not a cold-blooded assassin. He was a victim of his circumstances. After years of frustration, humiliation and disappointment, he pulled the trigger.

The provocations had been piling up.

According to his latest medical report that came a day before his death, Dipendra suffered from extremely high blood pressure, most likely hypertension. And he was just thirty. Dipendra's life was highly stressful and he faced a health risk that could have even threatened his life. He also suffered from high cholesterol levels and what seemed like an unusual fixation for food. The fixation could have been a symptom of deep-rooted insecurities picked up in infancy.

So what could have made the future king of Nepal—the flagbearer of the Shah dynasty—insecure?

It could be fact or fiction, but a web of predictions and prophecies that abound in the kingdom had drilled the fear into Dipendra's mind that Shah dynasty kings did not normally live beyond fifty years. His father, King Birendra, seemed to have defied those dark predictions by living to be fifty-five, the longest for a Shah king. But Dipendra himself cut short his father's life span with a short burst of a submachinegun.

According to Dipendra's closest friends, the crown prince often shared with them his deepest fears and frustrations. One of the biggest ones was: 'I am already thirty years old, and Shah dynasty kings don't live to be more than fifty.'

In what he perceived as his short remaining years, Dipendra had over-reaching expectations from himself. There was a long list of things he wanted to do, for himself and for his country. He was in a hurry. But he had always been thwarted in doing them—and he blamed one person, most of all, for blocking all his ambitions.

His mother, Queen Aiswarya.

Psychologists say that sons are generally mother-fixated, and that mothers play a very important role in their future psychological balance. In Dipendra's point of view, the queen was a doting mother—but only for his brother, Prince Nirajan, and his sister, Princess Shruti. For Dipendra, the rules seemed to be different, and the crown prince could never sense the reason for the apparent hostility his mother had towards him. He respected her, but her dominance gave him the feeling that he did not have control over his life.

Dipendra could not forget a patchwork of moments from the past: as when he was very sick and suffering from typhoid in the hostel of the Budhanilkantha School, and his hostel warden called the palace to let the queen know of the child's serious condition. The crown prince expected her to come running to his side. But when the queen hung up on the warden, the instructions were different and crisp: 'Take him to the school infirmary.'

Maybe Dipendra's parents wanted him to be tough, in preparation for being the king. Perhaps that is why the crown prince was gifted a real pistol on his eighth birthday, and several other weapons since, and the king wanted the crown prince to test all new weapons. Perhaps that stopped them from taking any corrective measures when he was caught selling liquor to other students at Eton. Perhaps that kept them from controlling their son's frightening obsession for the most lethal weapons available in the country. Perhaps that is why Queen Aiswarya—who was supposed to be the most nurturant figure in the life of the crown prince—wanted to control his very life.

Queen Aiswarya could be assertive and harsh. She could also be very creative and kind-hearted, but Dipendra believed that those sentiments were reserved for others, not him. Dipendra was looking for approval and acceptance from his parents. But his mother made him feel ordinary and unloved.

For several weeks, Dipendra had been having mood swings and stress disorders. He often threw tantrums. Devyani used to talk to him and calm him.

Dipendra had the deepest respect for his father, but his feelings for his mother seemed driven more by a sense of duty and his fear of her. There was a wall of frustrations between Dipendra and his mother. Psychologists say that a sensitive child—like Dipendra— normally suffers from high stress if the mother is a combination of being strong, powerful and strict.

Dipendra's life would be a lesson, but not for kings or statesmen. It would be a lesson for parents.

Bachelor at thirty: Nepal's most eligible bachelor was still single at thirty. In his part of the world, that was an age when an average male was married, with a couple of children. The reason for the bachelorhood was quite simple: his mother did not want him to marry the girl he liked, and he did not want to marry the girl his mother liked. At fifteen, Dipendra had fallen in love with the first girl he really got to know: Supriya Shah, the granddaughter of the queen mother's sister. By eighteen, he wanted to marry Supriya. The queen refused. A few years later, the question of his marriage was floating around, and his parents wanted him to get married with lawyer Garima Rana. They dated for some months, then realized they were not made for each other. They mutually decided to split. Then Dipendra fell in love with Devyani, and desperately wanted to marry her.

The queen refused again, but this time shocked the crown prince by asking him to marry the girl she had earlier rejected, Supriya Shah. Dipendra refused. His mother insisted that he should, and must, marry Supriya only.

The crown prince's anger was not over the opposition to his marriage with Devyani Rana. He was furious that *he was not being allowed to marry at all*. He had finally decided that he would marry her in the next wedding season, even if it meant defying the wishes of his parents.

It was a tussle between a tough mother and her tough son, both strong-headed warriors.

There were also other decisions that had deeply hurt Dipendra. In contrast with the decision not to let him marry, all his younger siblings were already married or engaged.

His younger sister, Princess Shruti, got married in May 1997. The ceremony was a grand affair, and funds were earmarked in the government's national budget for the celebration. Princess Shruti was strongly opposed to Dipendra's marriage with Devyani.

Prince Nirajan was already engaged to a girl called Ayushma Rana, and a wedding date was expected to be set soon, in view of the insistence from the girl's ailing mother. Dipendra's younger cousin, Prince Paras, was also married with a young daughter.

It seemed humiliating for Dipendra not to be allowed to choose a bride, despite being the crown prince, when all the siblings around him were married.

Unemployed at thirty: For a crown prince and at his age, Dipendra had very little to show for himself. His father had become king at twenty-six, and had control of the army even before that. But Dipendra believed he had been kept away from responsibilities all his life and never trusted enough to handle tough tasks. He had searched for years for approval and acceptance from his parents, but he seemed to never get it in the way he wanted and expected it.

According to his close friends, Dipendra was not satisfied just inaugurating festivals, accompanying his parents to official functions and being reduced to a mere showboy for Nepal's royalty. He had plans for his country, and his freedom and creativity had been stifled in such a way that he never got to attempt those plans.

He was trapped in a warp.

He was unable to complete his doctorate in geography due to family obstacles. He was unable to carry out his plan to computerize the palace and the army because the queen rejected the company he chose for the contract. His plans to modernize the army with modern weaponry and logistics had been thwarted for years.

According to one of his most intimate friends, Dipendra was 'terribly concerned about the Maoist insurgency and felt that it could only be resolved with a hearts-and-mind campaign'. He had not been asked in any way to help tackle the crisis, but the crown prince felt that the government needed to pump funds, in the areas worst affected by the rebellion, in social security projects, farming practices, and an education system. He believed this would allow the people of the affected areas to have an alternative source of development, and would wean them away from the insurgency.

He had ideas. He wasn't heard. He thought he was never taken seriously.

Dipendra was amazed to see how Lee Kuan Yew had changed Singapore in thirty years from a fishing village to a country with the world's ninth highest per capita income, and an almost negligible record of corruption and crime. When he brainstormed with friends, he felt that Nepal could also have similar achievements.

Despite his capabilities, his duties were mostly honorific. In the twelve years after his coming of age ceremony, his duties had involved making state visits to six countries and attending royal funerals or weddings in five. Over the past several years, Devyani had convinced him that he needed to spread out and try to use his talents in areas he liked. The result was the crown prince's widely appreciated leadership in the organization of the 1999 South Asian Federation Games.

The only time he was given some real power was when his father was abroad, when he officiated as the chairman of the council of royal representatives, which looked after the affairs of the state. When the king returned, it was back to inaugurations and youth festivals for the crown prince.

Unloved at thirty: He felt unloved by his family. The only person from whom Dipendra received unconditional love was Devyani, his ultimate stress-buster, who assumed the nurturant role in his life that originally belonged to his mother. Dipendra was also sometimes hurt that his father sided with his mother, rather than with him.

But Dipendra needed to feel wanted in his family, so he went out of his way in trying to care for everybody, an innocent attempt to win their approval. He believed that the love was never reciprocated.

Dipendra followed the palace grind and had lunch and dinner with his parents every day. He wrote a poem for his mother on her birthday. He declared that his mother, often slammed for her hardline views, had been made a scapegoat during the pre-democracy days, and was deeply disturbed when she was attacked with stones while going to the Pashupatinath temple during the 1990 campaign. He remained for days by his father's side when he suffered a heart attack and made arrangements for him to be flown to Britain. When his mother had a fall and seriously injured her hip and knee, Dipendra flew her in from Bharatpur town and was with her throughout the operation and stay in the Army Hospital. He visited the queen mother every evening, and did all her shopping, even for mundane things.

According to his closest friends, Dipendra had to take permission from his parents before he did anything—from official functions to permission to go out of the room. He never forgot their birthdays, Father's Day and Mother's Day. On such occasions, he bought them gifts and cards and cooked them their favourite dishes. When he returned from abroad, he would bring everybody presents—almost fifty members of the extended royal family.

There was little he got in return, except family hostility.

Title threatened at thirty: The queen was adamant that her son would not marry Devyani. Her reasons were astounding. Queen Aiswarya belonged to the Juddha Shumshere, one of the two rival branches of the powerful Rana clan. Devyani was a member of the rival Chandra Shumshere branch. But this seemed a shallow reason, because Garima Rana, the lady considered by the queen for a prospective daughter-in-law, was also a Chandra Shumshere Rana.

The queen reportedly also objected to Devyani's links with India, considering the strong opposition to India in parts of the Nepalese royal and government establishments. She also rejected the Scindia family of

Gwalior, which she said was inferior to her own Shah family. But Queen Aiswarya's own first cousin is married to a sister of Madhavrao Scindia, Devyani's uncle. And Prince Paras is also married to an Indian princess.

The queen struck the final nail when she started telling Dipendra, with the concurrence of the king, that he would not remain the crown prince if he married Devyani—that he would be provided all luxuries but not the status of the crown prince. Prince Nirajan, who the queen said would then be the crown prince, slammed the idea, but the queen's attitude caused deep hurt to Dipendra. Devyani seemed to make the queen insecure. Her strong domination over her son did not help.

But the man who was considered god was, in his intimate life, only human, with emotions and frustration and pain.

The crown prince went berserk after being in a seemingly calm, cheerful state during the Billiard Room party. A detailed psychological and physiological analysis shows that the most likely reason was that his deep inner conflict and his pent-up aggression, due to the given reasons, was manifested in what was apparently an acute psychotic attack. Narcotic substances including hashish and an unidentified black substance together magnified his hidden feelings suddenly and transformed them into violence. The exact catalyst for the psychotic attack—an unknown event or conversation during the day—is unknown, but it succeeded in triggering his most violent instinct.

Dipendra had crossed the thin line between sanity and insanity.

It was as if Stanley Ipkis, the character played by Jim Carey in *The Mask*, had worn the wooden mask and come face to face with a person whom he had secretly hated all his life but never dared to say so. In a snap, all the fragile backstage feelings poured out, engulfing the person and several others too.

Dipendra appears to have been a man of intense emotions, a person who wanted to prove himself, who was seeking unconditional love and support. He wanted to have control over his life.

Pointers

His face was expressionless. This lends credence to the theory that it was a psychotic attack. He showed complete apathy when he killed his immediate family.

He remained speechless throughout the massacre.

According to studies, psychosis develops over time but might manifest itself suddenly. Given the precipitating factors in Dipendra's life, this is what seems to have happened.

In the afternoon, he seemed highly agitated, going by the way he was driving after lunch. The behaviour of the day could hold a key to the behaviour in the evening.

He killed his father at close range, firing on three occasions, but did not shoot the queen point-blank when he was walking backwards. Queen Aiswarya was shot from the back. Studies say that a son in awe of his mother does not show direct hostility towards her when there is a deep conflict between getting her love and fulfilling her demands. In such situations, psychologists say, the son hates everybody who allows her to have her way.

Even in his frenzied state, he spared Prince Paras and Dr Rajiv Shahi—and it might be more than a coincidence that they were the ones who supported his plans to marry Devyani.

The one person who could have diverted the rage and soothed him—Devyani—had not met him that day.

The Psychoanalyst's View

Keeping in view the highly stressful conditions that became heightened in the last few weeks before Dipendra's death, perhaps the crown prince heard something very traumatic which must have caused him anxiety and anger, because his needs were thwarted. The use of alcohol and the drugs might have exaggerated the distress to trigger an acute psychosis.

Following is a sampling of some psychological studies that support the view that Dipendra, pushed to the corner by a history of deep frustrations, finally snapped when his ego defence system broke and he suffered the attack:

The majority of adults with and without psychiatric disorders, who commit aggressive acts, are more likely to commit such acts against familiar persons, usually family members.

Many drugs can cause the acute onset of a temporary psychosis. Many clinicians also feel that the use of illicit drugs can precipitate a schizophrenic or psychotic episode.

Hashish, the resin obtained from the leaves of the cannabis or hemp plant, is considered six times stronger than marijuana. The major effects of hashish include changes in mood, alertness, and cognition. The most typical psychological effect is an elevation of mood, associated with the decreased capacity to accurately gauge the passage of time, intensification of perceptions, inappropriate manifestations of emotions, passivity, apathy and drowsiness.

But in some cases, users may become acutely paranoid and in individuals with a history of precipitating factors for schizophrenia, even the use of marijuana may trigger an onset of the symptoms.

All the emotions are magnified.

Psychologists say the family and its behaviour is also often responsible for such attacks. According to one model, stiff interactions usually occur between a parent and the potentially schizophrenic offspring. A parent might avoid a physical embrace, yet say: 'Why don't you show me more affection?' It is a 'damned-if-you-do and damned-if-you-don't' situation in which the offspring or child feels emotionally paralysed.

Parental behaviour that brings the onset of psychotic attacks includes criticism, attempt to control offspring's life and inadequate support. The crown prince went through all of these, according to his closest friends.

If the 'black substance' was a strong stimulant narcotic drug, it could be possible that it heightened his internal turmoil. There are psychostimulants available which, if taken, can lead to extremely exaggerated emotional outbursts among users.

Chapter Eight

The Corridors of History

AJATSHATRU. SITTING IN the breezy classrooms of the Budhanilkantha School, Crown Prince Dipendra had read in his history books about the ancient prince whose father Bimbisara had ruled over Nepal and parts of eastern India centuries ago, when the Buddha walked these parts of the earth. Ajatshatru's Lichhavi dynasty had preceded Dipendra's Shah dynasty by almost twenty-five centuries; they stood at opposite ends of a massive time capsule—and yet, they suddenly seemed like two identical, hot-blooded young men.

Prince Ajatshatru had killed his father, King Bimbisara. Soon after the prince brought the sharp-edged dagger down on the stunned monarch, he was king.

Crown Prince Dipendra had brought down his stunned father in a pool of blood. Within hours, as he lay in a cobweb of life support systems, he too, ironically, was being appointed king.

As Nepal woke up on that Saturday morning, it seemed like a nation on its knees—mourning for its king, confused over what to think of its crown prince, terrified about its future, furious at its government. The

dark, silent evening of the previous day, when Nepal
had a seemingly happy royal family, and the sunny
morning of 2 June, seemed centuries away. Thousands
of telephones were ringing across the valley, as people
broke the news to others and spread the shock, but the
telephone calls meant much more to 125 men and
women, who had been woken up in their homes across
the city by the news, much before the others. These
were the revered members of the Raj Parishad, the
Privy Council, which looked after affairs of the palace.
Once in several decades, it also performed another
crucial task—it chose and named the king of Nepal.

That moment had come.

Today the council had a tough task on its hands.
The man who many said had killed the kingdom's
monarch lay senseless on a hospital bed in a heavily
guarded chamber. He was the assassin. He was also the
successor of the man he had killed. He was the destiny
of his tiny Himalayan nation.

Kamal Shah's hands trembled as she kept the receiver
in her Lazimpeth home back on its cradle. Then she
became the steely woman she had been in decades of
public life. She was a member of the Privy Council. The
voice at the other end belonged to a senior council
official.

Dipendra had to be named king. Soon.

The council's task seemed to belong to the moment—
the quick reaction by a group of sane men and women
after what seemed an insane, brutal murder. But it was
much more than that. The council was set to name the
successor to the ancient throne of Nepal. It was a sacred
task that had long centuries of tradition and history
behind it in the world's only Hindu monarchy, whose

origins were veiled in mystery.

Nepal's earliest known historical event seems to be an invasion from the eastern part of the country by the warlike Kiratas around 700 B.C. A millennium later, close to A.D. 300, the Lichhavis sought to take over Nepal, swarming in from the northern Indian plains. The Lichhavis were Hindus, but they were to encourage the multicultural diversity that became the hallmark of modern Nepal, with their patronage of Buddhists. While Ajatshatru's dynasty became famous by the patricide, it also amazed the Chinese with its architectural marvels. The Lichhavis' trump card: control of the route that meandered through the Himalayas from India to Tibet, and was used extensively for trade. Centuries later, a determined man on horseback would escape Potala Palace in Tibet after his failed uprising against the Chinese through the same route, to take refuge in India. This monk, known to the world as the Dalai Lama, would be followed by tens of thousands of other gutsy monks in flowing red robes, sneaking past Chinese border guards.

The Lichhavis also started creating a political balance by marrying off their daughters to potential rivals—an example followed by successive dynasties in India. The Lichhavi Princess Bhrikuti became the wife of Tibet's King Srongsan Gampo. It was an example that has also been followed to the modern era by Nepal's monarchy. Members of the Shah dynasty married into the powerful Rana clan to maintain a balance of power and avoid hostility. King Birendra Bir Bikram Shah Dev had married a Rana girl, who became Nepal's powerful queen, revered as a goddess. Queen Aiswarya Rajya Lakshmi Devi Shah wanted to similarly maintain the balance, and had for years decided to make Supriya, her niece and the daughter of a powerful military general, her daughter-in-law and her successor as the Queen of Nepal.

That key question, and perhaps only that insistence, would become the cause of the multiple assassinations that wiped out the royal family.

But back to history, where the Lichhavis' reign was coming to an end around the eighth century, sucking the kingdom into the vortex of a dark era. Rulers came, but they were more of invaders occupying the throne while they exploited the nation's riches. As in several other parts of what later became South Asia, marauders burned down homes and looted whatever booty they could lay their hands on. Lawlessness prevailed in several parts. On the positive side, Kathmandu and Bhaktapur, cities with pagoda-like temples, exquisite architecture and narrow pathways that are now part of the kingdom's ancient heritage, sprung up. The cult of Tantra came into its own. The living goddess, the teenage Kumari, was establishing her own kingdom of faith, often with a following only second to the king himself.

The Malla dynasty followed. Soon there would be three kingdoms in Nepal—Kathmandu, Bhaktapur and Patan. The trophy for all of them was the trade route to Tibet, for which they continuously squabbled.

Centuries passed. By the 1700s, the Kathmandu Valley was prosperous. The kingdom was thriving. It attracted a swarm of visitors. Missionaries. Kashmiri traders. Hindu priests. Sorcerers. Mercenaries. Buddhist gurus. With wealth came greed—and enemies.

The three cities became the target of formidable

rivals in their vicinity, including the Gorkhalis in the central expanse of the country. The mountain town of Gorkha was home to the Shah dynasty that was destined to rule Nepal through most of its modern times. Prithvinarayan Shah had eyes on Kathmandu. Centuries before the time of the slain King Birendra, one of his valiant forefathers was waiting for the right moment to make the strike on Kathmandu Valley.

Prithvinarayan Shah had ambition and determination. It helped that he also had something no other rival had—guns.

It was an auspicious morning in 29 September 1768 when he made the final assault. He was helped in many ways by the stunned man on the throne—a man seen as a lustful drunkard, slave of the libido—King Jayaprakash. According to legend, he was so lustful that he started desiring a goddess he had long worshipped, with whom he used to play dice. Then the powerful goddess, Taleju, parted ways. The infuriated Taleju threatened Jayaprakash that his kingdom was doomed, unless he recognized a young girl, who would be called the living goddess or Kumari, as her reincarnation. The terrified Jayaprakash instituted the festival in which the living goddess was taken around the city in a caparisoned chariot, with the king and his subjects seeking the blessings of the Kumari. The wrathful Taleju, whom Jayaprakash had wrongly lusted for, is revered even today.

Then, the army of Prithvinarayan Shah, inching closer to Kathmandu, made the final swoop. It was the day of the chariot procession of the living goddess, the Kumari Jatra day. Jayaprakash escaped from his kingdom, leaving behind a motley group of drunken soldiers too engrossed in revelry to fight the formidable and determined attackers. He would return later to die at the Pashupatinath temple.

Kathmandu was taken without a fight. As the kingdom swiftly changed hands, thousands of people were busy dancing and cheering as they worshipped the goddess. Prithvinarayan Shah ordered his soldiers to let the festivities continue. He walked up to the goddess and the Kumari made the ceremonial mark, the 'tika,' on his forehead. The Kumari had set off a tradition that would be followed even centuries later by the slain King Birendra.

The ceremony marked the social, cultural and religious amalgamation of the country's rainbow traditions under one figurehead, the king.

The Shah dynasty was in business.

Prithvinarayan Shah achieved supreme power, and made the greatest contribution to uniting Nepal as a country. By the time his reign ended in 1775, the kingdom's boundaries had become firmer and the army was more organized and stronger. Its weapons were bought from British India, and the fledgling mountain kingdom had started taking on the challenge of mighty armies in its neighbourhood: the Chinese in Tibet and the British colonial rulers in India. The borders were expanded to far beyond Nepal's traditional frontiers. The Shah rulers banished all foreigners from their territory—those who joined the exodus included traders from India and other countries, Roman Catholic missionaries, religious teachers, musicians, painters and singers.

Then they took on the might of the East India Company, now ruling India, and managed to stave off the onslaught. But Nepal lost substantial territory and pride after the Anglo-Nepalese War of 1814–16: the Treaty of Sagauli signed after the last battle saw the Shah kingdom lose Sikkim, now part of India's northeast, the territories of Kumaon and Garhwal, the lower Himalayan reaches now in the Indian state of Uttaranchal, and several other areas. Nepal's king also had to accept a British Resident, a symbolic humiliation for the country that never accepted British suzerainty, and had shut itself to all foreigners. But the palace struck back in a clever, subtle way: the British envoy was given a house on a piece of land that the local people believed was haunted. The Britisher got poor water supply, and poor services. His movements were restricted and government spies kept a close watch on him and the people he met with.

But Nepal would become a close friend of the British by the middle of the nineteenth century, mainly due to the help the royal army would extend to the colonial attempt to end the rebellion of 1857 in India.

Meanwhile, the royal saga that continued was laced with court squabbles and lust for power.

King Birendra's blood would not be the first of a royal to be spilled in Nepal's palace. On 25 April 1806, ruler Rana Bahadur Shah had a furious quarrel with his half-brother Sher Bahadur, watched by horrified courtiers, in the royal court. Blinded by rage, Sher Bahadur unleashed his sword and killed Rana Bahadur Shah before the gathering. Within minutes, he was also killed by a guard standing nearby. A former administrator called Bhimsen Thapa became prime minister, plotting with his junior queen, Tripurasundari, to quickly massacre ninety-three of their enemies.

Factional fighting followed after Thapa's death. Enemies were executed, with or without trial. And more killings were also about to take place within the palace.

Fateh Jang Chautaria, a prime minister in name but a king for all practical purposes, took over in November 1840. The prime minister preferred the advice of the queens to that of his cabinet. In January 1843, he formally declared that Lakshmidevi, one of the junior queens, would henceforth be his top adviser on affairs of the state, overruling even his eldest son Surendra Chautaria. The queen, meanwhile, was plotting to enthrone one of her own sons.

Mathbar Singh Thapa, the next prime minister, took over in December 1843. Two years later, on 17 May 1845, Queen Lakshmidevi allegedly engineered a palace coup in which Thapa was assassinated on her orders by Jang Bahadur Kunwar, his nephew and later the founder of the century-long Rana rule in the country.

The killing ended the era of the aristocracy in Nepal, and paved the way for the dictatorship of the prime ministers.

But not before another court massacre, one of the most devastating in Nepal's royal history until the annihilation of King Birendra's family.

Helped by the scheming junior queen, Fateh Jang Chautaria was back as the head of state in September 1845. But the real power behind the throne was a man called Gagan Singh, her favourite and apparently her lover, who commanded a far greater backing in the royal army than the king himself.

The palace was rife with plots and counterplots. On 14 September 1846, Gagan Singh was found killed in the palace. The stunned queen wanted revenge. She ordered an army commander to organize an immediate assembly of the top officials of the army and the palace, and their closest followers, in the palace armoury, 'kot' in Nepali.

Tension swept through the corridors of power. Colonels and courtiers walked in; so did lobbyists and power brokers, spies and royal rumourmongers. The queen tried to whip up hysteria at the assembly, blaming the rival Pande clan in an emotional speech. She demanded that the prime minister execute the Pande leader, whom she accused of carrying out her favourite's murder. Suddenly, fighting broke out in the crowd. Rival camps emerged. Swords and daggers were drawn. Not surprisingly, Jang Bahadur, the alleged assassin of the previous prime minister, was the only nobleman in the melée with an organized troop formation ready to strike. They started slicing away at their opponents. In less than an hour, the courtyard was splattered with the bodies of royals, other nobles and their followers. The gloss of Nepal's nobility had been wiped out in a single slaughter. On the next day, Jang Bahadur Kunwar, later given the title of 'Rana' by the king, was the new prime minister of Nepal.

The Rana era had started.

For more than a century, the Shah kings became the puppets—and palace prisoners—of the Rana prime ministers. The Ranas' guards restricted the movements of the kings, and no one except the king's immediate family could meet him without the prime minister's permission. To maintain his symbolic supremacy, however, the king was addressed as 'maharajadhiraj' (emperor of emperors), and would be greeted by using the honorific 'shri' five times before his name. The Rana would be addressed by using 'shri' three times. The name of Nepal's king is prefixed even now with 'shri paanch'.

Jang Bahadur also started a tradition that has continued up to the current king—of relation by marriage between the Shah and the Rana clans. It was a virtual guarantee for maintaining political stability in the kingdom. The first such relation was formalized in 1854, when his eight-year eldest son Jagat Jang married the six-year-old daughter of Surendra Bikram Shah.

In the Rana household, history was winding its way towards another assassination. Jang Bahadur's successor was his elder brother Ranoddip Singh, a childless and elderly man who became prime minister in 1877. Conspiracies flew thick as Jang Bahadur's sons plotted a way to snatch power and, in 1885, assassinated the frail Ranoddip Singh.

One more body had fallen in Nepal's corridors of power. It would not be the last.

By the late 1940s, Nepal's titular monarch was King Tribhuvan Bir Bikram Shah Dev, a gutsy man who had for long been openly opposing the Ranas. His titular status was about to change.

Through the power squabbles of centuries, Nepal's people had been going through tough times. Soon there was so much misrule and discontent that the nation seemed sitting on the edge of a revolution, similar to the countrywide campaign that would soon set India free of British bondage.

Protests against the Ranas started in 1950. Political parties were thriving, although officially there was still a ban on them. The number of demonstrators was swelling. Thousands of people had stepped on the streets, demanding the return of the king's rule. In India, colonial rule had been replaced by a democracy under the republic's first prime minister, Jawaharlal Nehru, whose sympathies lay with the man in the Narayanhiti Palace, King Tribhuvan, rather than the autocratic Ranas.

As the country was drowned in a wave of demonstrations and furious campaigns, King Birendra escaped from the palace and sought asylum in the Indian Embassy in Kathmandu, the largest diplomatic mission in the country. It was 6 November 1950. Soon a car was speeding towards the airport. It belonged to the Indian ambassador and had an unlikely passenger— the king, the great-grandfather of Crown Prince Dipendra, who fled to India.

In the outlying towns and villages, an armed revolution was brewing, aided by underground activists of political parties. In New Delhi, the Rana ruler had started negotiations with the Indian government, and promised to restore real power to the king. He ceded power on 8 January 1951. The king made a triumphant return to Kathmandu. In February, a new ministry was sworn in.

After a century of bondage, the Shah dynasty was back in power.

Nepal started opening up to the outside world. Tourists and mountaineers started streaming in, drawn by the magic of the highest peak in the world, Mt. Everest, and several other lofty ranges.

King Tribhuvan died in 1954, and was succeeded by his son, Crown Prince Mahendra. In 1962, King Mahendra took away Parliament's powers and gave to his people absolute monarchy, and the Panchayat system that was aimed at locally disseminating power. Political parties remained banned.

In 1972, King Birendra took over the throne, and succeeded in retaining his people's reverence for the monarchy.

King Birendra's Nepal straddled modernity and Western influences on one side, and tradition and superstition on the other. He had draped his kingdom, his monarchy and his family in the centuries-old beliefs—common, perhaps, even to the reign of a Shah dynasty king two centuries ago—but he made sure that the sights, sounds and colours of the twenty-first century always made their way through that veil. That set the king apart from his contemporary in the neighbouring mountain kingdom of Bhutan, King Jigme Singye Wangchuk.

This meshing of tradition and modernity meant that Nepal's Britain-educated crown prince would sit with his religious family at common prayers and visit the royal priest, but on a breezy evening, he would also drive in his Pajero to the pizza joint on Durbar Marg for a bite with his friends.

But some would say the kingdom was weighed down by too many beliefs and superstitions, much too many for a monarchy that had already gingerly stepped past the threshold into a new millennium. As with any other nation, Nepal has its share of folklore.

Like the Yeti, the 'abominable snowman'. The mysterious giant, elusive creature that seems to exist only in the minds of Nepal's mystery-minded and the bleary-eyed mountaineers climbing its jagged peaks. Or the Toothache Tree near the Bangemuda Square in the city, where those squealing in pain after a visit to the dentist can go for solace: tap a coin hard enough on the slab of wood there, and the god of healing will put the smile back on your face! And beware when you step into a traditional Nepali building built in the ancient Newari style: the staircase must climb towards only the east, west or south, never the north, because that is the direction of the earth in which the departed souls go after death.

In Bhaktapur, wooden poles used by priests for the ritual processions have to be put through an elaborate procedure before they can be used, or else they will break during the processions, under the gaze of thousands. The priest saunters into the nearby forest with a black goat and walks around, waiting for it to bang either its head or posterior into a tree. When it does, that tree becomes the chosen tree, sawed for the festival poles by devotees.

Hundreds of such quaint beliefs pepper the lives of the people. Women with tattoos of flowers on their feet can be sure of exchanging the marks for food when they die and go to heaven. A crow never dies a natural death, it has to be killed. People do not die of snakebite because there is no poison in the snake's fangs—they die of the poisonous tears that the repentant snakes pour on the victims.

Those who believe in demons, beware: many are believed to be floating around in the Kathmandu Valley. Some appear with the seasons and creep into their victims' lungs and intestines, causing them cough, cold, gastric troubles and tummy aches. Others, like the ferocious but stupid *rakshasa*, are permanent residents. He can chomp away a full-bodied man at a single go, but can still be beaten by anyone with just an ounce of brain (that's much more than what the massive demon has). But the most deadly of all seems to be the seductive, sadistic and beautiful *kichikinni*, with her feet twisted backwards like all demons worth their salt. She seduces men by squealing like a monkey and calling her victim to lonely areas—where she lets her victim die with a smile on his face. She tickles them to death, they say.

Dozens of such ancient beliefs and curses were floating in Kathmandu's mournful air in the days after the massacre. One such was the prophecy that the Hindu god Gorakh Nath made to the valiant King Prithvinarayan Shah, the Shah era founder, as he prepared to attack and take the capital from Jayaprakash. According to legend, on the morning of 29 September 1768, as the Shah king prepared to order the final assault into the valley, Gorakh Nath appeared before him, disguised as a hermit. The king offered curd to the sage. Gorakh Nath, according to the legend, swallowed the curd, threw it up and offered it back to the king. Prithvinarayan Shah found this repulsive and threw the curd on the ground, bathing his own feet in white. The guru was furious: he told the king that he could have had all his wishes fulfilled if he had swallowed his pride—and the curd. But he had spurned it, and Gorakh Nath uttered a curse that would ring through the centuries: since the king had thrown the curd on his ten fingers, his dynasty would not live beyond ten generations after Prithvinarayan Shah.

King Birendra Bir Bikram Shah Dev was the eleventh Shah monarch.

The Shah dynasty did not end with him and Nepal had three kings in four days, King Dipendra and King Gyanendra being the twelfth and thirteenth respectively.

But it seemed that in keeping with the ominous prophecy, the glory of the Shah monarchy had died with King Birendra.

Other rumours, beliefs and ominous prophecies did the rounds of Kathmandu. Amid rumours that the crown prince picked up his weapons over the question of his marriage and the queen's stalling his union with his beloved, many tradition-minded Nepalese were reminded of a piece of astrological advice that royal priests are said to have given to the king and queen: that the crown prince should not be allowed to marry until he was thirty-five, or else the king would die.

Yet others would say that this prophecy would not have held anyway against another dark astrological prediction, one of those beliefs that spring from unknown sources and spread through word of mouth: that no king of Nepal would live beyond fifty-five years. Supporters of this theory backed it with what they said was evidence of its credibility. It has been proved wrong only once since 1768. Only King Rajendra Bir Bikram Shah Dev died at sixty-eight.

King Birendra celebrated his fifty-fifth birthday on 28 December 2000, Nepal's national day, and many people were relieved that the prophecy had been proved wrong. But their beliefs seemed reaffirmed on the morning of 2 June 2001.

King Prithvinarayan Shah was fifty-two when he died, and his successors Pratap Singh Shah, Rana Bahadur Shah and Girvana Yuddha Bikram Shah passed away at 26, 31 and 19 years. The prophecy became entrenched with King Rajendra's successor Surendra Bikram Shah, who died at 52, Trailokya Bikram Shah at 30, Prithvi Bir Bikram Shah at 36. In the twentieth century, King

Birendra's grandfather, King Tribhuvan, died at 48 and his father King Mahendra at 52.

But no prophecy, no blessing, and no guru had prepared Nepal for what happened.

Chapter Nine

Aftermath

THE LARGE, HIGH-CEILINGED room in the Narayanhiti Palace hummed with the low murmur of exhausted conversation. The ashtray brimmed with cigarette stubs. The waste basket was full. A bunch of confidential papers trembled on the large wooden table with every sweep of an old ceiling fan. The small group of officials in the palace secretariat had worked hard through the night. They had driven into the palace compound soon after word of the massacre started filtering out of the palace. By dawn, they had drafted and redrafted several times a statement declaring that King Birendra had died.

They waited. They could not tell the ccuntry yet. The law forbade the announcement before his successor was named.

But the country was getting to know, anyway. Despite the veil of secrecy over the events of the previous night, two newspapers had managed to bring out special editions with the story. For thousands of people, the first word of the tragedy was, ironically, from outside the country—from shocked expatriates who had started calling their homes around midnight.

Thousands sat glued to their television screens, watching breaking news on BBC and CNN. The state-run and private channels quickly yanked all programmes off air, showing only still images of the royal palace, with mournful music playing in the background. The same tunes were being played on the radio, and listeners heard them in homes, in taxis, inside shops in hidden alleys and in hotels.

The roads were suddenly deserted, except for policemen in blue, holding wooden truncheons, and the police vans patrolling the roads. Shops opened, but the shutters were fast coming down. At the Narayanhiti Palace, it seemed nothing had happened: the military police guards stood as stoically as on any other day. Slowly, thousands of people started stepping out of their homes and walking towards the palace in a silent, directionless procession. Near the palace gates, many just squatted on the roadsides. Many dispersed to go home and help their families grapple with the overwhelming tragedy.

In several national capitals across Asia, journalists of international media organizations had also been woken up by late night calls from their offices. They were scrambling now to get onto the first available flights into Kathmandu.

Close to 9 a.m. in the capital, crowds watched as a caravan of expensive foreign-made cars started driving into the campus that housed a huge white-washed building with large pagoda-like roofs. The building housed the office of the Raj Parishad or the Privy Council, which would name the new king. Apart from the 125 members of the council nominated by the king, it had most top leaders of the country, including the prime minister, all the members of his cabinet, the chief justice of the Supreme Court, the Parliament Speaker. Army guards screened visitors into the campus.

Only about 70 Privy Council members had been able to come at the short notice; the rest were out of town on the weekend. The members trooped in silently into the 200-seat first floor hall, adorned by large framed pictures of ten Shah dynasty kings that similar congregations had named earlier. Prime Minister Girija Prasad Koirala, several of his predecessors, opposition party leaders, royal family relatives and other top leaders took their seats on the first of the several rows of chairs. Keshar Jang Rayamajhi, the council's chairman, cleared his throat and started the most difficult council session of his career. Rayamajhi formally informed the members about what they already knew about the massacre, as well as what the doctors had informed him at the hospital: the crown prince was still alive.

Several members spoke. The proceedings continued for almost two hours. No councilman objected to the installation of Dipendra as the new king. At approximately 11 a.m., state radio interrupted the strains of mournful music and Rayamajhi's voice rang out: 'With the deepest regret, I have to inform you that His Majesty King Birendra Bir Bikram Shah Dev died last night at 2115 hours. According to the grand traditions, we declare that His Majesty's eldest son, Crown Prince Dipendra Bir Bikram Shah Dev, will be the King of Nepal as of six o'clock in the evening 20 Jyestha 2058. Since the king is invalid and is mentally and physically unfit to carry out his responsibilities, His Highness Prince Gyanendra shall be the regent.'

But Nepal was not told what had caused the king's

death. It was the country's worst-kept secret—it was out on the streets but the establishment was not ready to say it. There was a reason: the eyewitnesses had identified Dipendra as the killer but the law had named him the king—and according to the same law, pointing a finger at the king would constitute an act of treason. For the moment, the cause of the king's death was kept under wraps.

But outside the palace and the Privy Council office, not many knew, or would buy, this logic. It was slowly getting ugly on the streets. People wanted to be told. They wanted to disbelieve the foreign news channels that were already blaming their beloved crown prince for the killings.

In another part of the city, a young woman was stepping out of her home, Bijay Baas, in a trance, accompanied by distressed family members as she got into a car that headed towards the airport. Devyani Rana had for long received threatening calls. Media reports were now claiming that the crown prince carried out the killings only because he was not allowed to marry the woman he loved. After the events of Friday night and the blame game that was about to start, her safety seemed in deep peril. The traumatized Devyani was soon seated in an Indian Airlines plane, headed for New Delhi.

The man on her mind was still in the intensive care unit of the military hospital, occasionally responding with a cough or by gently shaking his feet when pinched. The storm of the previous evening had settled down now. The bodies of the king, queen and the other victims were being prepared for the funeral, to be held later in the day. Inside the operation theatre, plastic surgeons were working on the disjointed fingers of his aunt, Princess Shobha Shahi.

Since the truth was not coming out from the palace, it was time for the conspiracy theories to tumble out. Nepal's rumour factories, which frequently harm people or cause unrest by spreading panic and discontent, had their biggest assignment at hand. They blamed Prince Gyanendra for the massacre, raising questions about his absence at the Friday night dinner. They pointed fingers at the Indian intelligence agency, the Research and Analysis Wing, or RAW. They claimed the killings were carried out by America's CIA in an operation it had purportedly planned for three years.

The people's anger was also directed against Prince Gyanendra's son, the twenty-seven-year-old Prince Paras. He was among those targeted in the conspiracy theories. Married to an Indian princess and father of a young daughter, Paras was widely seen in Nepal as someone who had caused deep embarrassment to his father and King Birendra by repeatedly grabbing the headlines for the wrong reasons. Some said he was the second-generation version of the king's brother Dhirendra. Paras was accused of involvement in a hit-and-run case which killed a hugely popular singer, Pravin Gurung. Gurung's death sparked widespread anger among the Nepalese youth, especially because an ordinary soldier owned up the accident at a police station and the story was seen as an attempt to silence the opposition against the prince. In August 2000, as many as 600,000 signatures were collected and forwarded to the king, seeking action against Paras. The king came close to taking action, but never did.

One palace official said of him: 'Paras is a very nice

guy, when he chooses to be.'

By 4 p.m., when the funeral was scheduled to begin, it seemed all of Kathmandu was out on the roads. There were people peeping from rooftops and window ledges and huddled on any inch of space they found—even treetops and the roofs of temples.

Wails rent the air as the waiting crowds caught the first glimpse of their royal family. Then, the anger started pouring out.

'Hang the killers of the king!' a young man screamed. Others joined him, raising their fists in anger, screaming slogans against Prime Minister Koirala. Stones started raining on Koirala's car, smashing its windows. The prime minister escaped unhurt and was shielded by his guards. Stampedes occurred at several points in the miles-long procession. As the mobs started getting unruly, soldiers fired several times in the air to prevent the violence spreading to anywhere near the funeral procession.

But the first stone had been lobbed. And the anger would only be ignited further by the flames that raged that night on the eight funeral pyres besides the muddy waters of the Bagmati River, in the shadow of the Pashupatinath temple.

It might remain a big-time journalism mystery: if reporters had translated one word correctly that Sunday morning, could Nepal have been saved from much of the violence that was to follow?

The new regent, Prince Gyanendra, issued a statement soon after taking over, giving the first official version of what had happened on Friday night. It had been a tricky statement to prepare for the press secretariat.

They could not describe the right cause of the killings without calling Dipendra the killer; and they could not describe Dipendra as the killer because he was the king and above reproach.

If Gyanendra had named his nephew, the new king, in the massacre, the regent would technically be committing an act of sedition against the monarch. That also meant that even if he wanted to, Gyanendra could not order any sort of inquiry into the incident to satisfy the public hunger for information. In effect, the palace, bound by the Constitution, was not in a position to say anything about the massacre.

After agonizing for long over the vexed constitutional position, the press secretariat issued a terse, vaguest-possible statement, which quoted Gyanendra as saying that the killings were caused by 'a sudden discharge of an automatic weapon'. Palace officials thought the statement would give the people something to chew on, and the next step would be decided once Dipendra's condition became clear.

No such luck.

Although Gyanendra never said so, journalists translating the statement amazingly described the Nepalese word '*aakasmik*'—sudden—as 'accidental'. The breaking news was out: Gyanendra had described the massacre as an accident. The regent was widely ridiculed in news stories. The wrong translation of one word turned the meaning of Gyanedra's statement upside down. It was baffling that the wrong translation was used across the board, from Nepalese newspapers, to global television networks.

Thousands who were in mourning were now furious at Gyanendra for calling the carnage 'an accident'. It seemed the ultimate humiliation, a scornful act from a prince whom an overwhelming number of people would continue to see as a conspirator in the murders.

Meanwhile, a car was pulling up at the residence of one of the cousins of Dipendra. Mrs Usha Rana, mother of Devyani Rana, walked past the soldiers at the posh villa and into the drawing room to meet a lady who was one of the best friends of Devyani. After the massacre, it was the first contact between the royal family and a member of Devyani's family. Devyani was being blamed for the massacre, and her mother had come to try and clear the air.

The nation was going ahead with its mourning rituals. Tens of thousands of people shaved their hair as a mark of bereavement. Barbers performed their task free of cost.

Some other heads were shaven too.

As darkness fell on the night of 2 June, Kathmandu Valley was set to receive several thousand such visitors. According to the security forces, Maoist political activists were streaming into the capital, shouting slogans in support of the king, with their heads shaven like thousands of other mourners. They were coming in from remote areas with a clear aim: spreading unrest, whipping up public passions against the monarchy. The time seemed right for the Maoists to try and win over the hearts of the people, whose love for the monarchy had so far prevented them from endorsing the Maoist revolution in several parts of the country. Several activists had written instructions on how to go about spreading unrest in the capital. In a daring act, others would publicly distribute fliers outside the main Southern Gate of the Narayanhiti Palace, calling the regent the 'villain' of the palace massacre.

Gyanendra, had been closely monitoring the condition of the new king. Dr Shrestha drove to the regent's residence every evening with a report on the condition of Dipendra, as well as those injured, including Gyanendra's wife, Princess Komal.

On the evening of Sunday, 3 June, Dr Shrestha's report had the foreboding of another tragedy. King Dipendra's health had worsened, and the doctors' team had held a meeting of the medical board. The verdict was clear: Dipendra was slipping into the brain dead zone.

The chances? Gyanendra asked.

Zero.

The doctors wanted to know what the royal family wanted them to do: with their consent, pull the plug, or let him die a natural death, trying to treat him until his heart stopped beating. Gyanendra checked with the queen mother, and returned to the doctor.

'Since there is a constitutional crisis, let nature take its own course,' he said. Dr Shrestha returned.

But there wasn't much else that the doctors could do.

At 3:30 a.m., Dipendra's heartbeat stopped. The ICU went into a tizzy. Doctors struggled hard for a long time, trying to revive him. But Nepal's most short-lived king had already slipped away into history, after a reign of less than 48 hours—all of it spent on a hospital bed in a maze of life support systems.

A terse medical bulletin followed: 'His Majesty King Dipendra Bir Bikram Shah Dev developed progressive slowing of the heartbeat this morning at 2:30 a.m. Resuscitative measures were instituted. Despite these measures, cardiac arrest occured at 3:30 a.m. from which His Majesty could not be revived.'

Next morning, the royal Privy Council met again, and this time the decision was much easier: since King Dipendra was unmarried and had no son or grandson to succeed him, the line of succession had been changed and Regent Prince Gyanendra would be the new king.

It was a homecoming for King Gyanendra. Among Nepal's oldtimers, a hundreds memories came swarming.

As a child, he had earlier been king briefly in 1950, when his grandfather, King Tribhuvan, fled to India with his family to plot a coup against Rana rule. Beneath a colourful, bejewelled canopy held by a turbaned palace guard, three-year-old Gyanendra had innocently walked to the throne, holding the hand of the prime minister, Mohan Shumshere Rana. Behind the young king in gilded clothes were dozens of courtiers, several wearing lookalikes of the long, plumed Shah crown. Gyanendra was enthroned in the courtyard of the Hanuman Dhoka palace.

Walking a few steps behind the king at the 1950 enthronement ceremony was a smart boy in a jacket and a black cap, called Pashupati Shumshere Rana. Half a century later, the name of his daughter would be a very familiar one in Nepal: Devyani Rana.

Gyanendra was king for all of four months. King Tribhuvan returned soon, and his young grandson, who had been named his successor, was forgotten in history— for then.

Close to 11 a.m., Gyanendra walked into the same cobbled courtyard where he had been brought five decades ago, to the old Shah dynasty palace called Hanuman Dhoka. The ancient golden throne, used for more than two centuries for royal enthronements, had been placed on a stone platform. The wooden structure of the old palace loomed above. Gyanendra, his head shaven, sat on the throne, with a gold image of the Sheshnaga, the nine-headed mythical serpent, arched behind his head.

As a gentle drizzle started, Keshari Raj Pandey, the chief royal priest, walked up to the platform, putting aside his walking stick, and placed the Shah dynasty crown, with a jewel-studded base and a long cream plume, on Gyanendra's head.

The emotionless King Gyanendra then walked out of the palace to a waiting chariot, drawn by cavalry soldiers atop six horses. Tensions soared as the chariot pulled out of the Durbar Square, into the streets where traffic had been blocked an hour ahead of the ceremony. No one clapped or cheered. Most just stared into open space, not even raising their folded hands in greeting. In side streets, hundreds of protesters were pushed back as they tried to surge towards the royal entourage.

It seemed that Nepal's monarchy had suddenly become distant from its people. Almost as soon as the new king entered his palace, riots broke out across the city.

Hundreds of youth pelted police with stones, burned tyres and swarmed the roads as police fired tear gas, and then real bullets, to quell the demonstrators. At least two people were killed and twenty wounded. A curfew was soon imposed and orders issued to shoot people after one warning. It was not an auspicious start for a king.

Hours later, an open army truck raced down the hill from the military hospital. A body draped in white shook inside as the truck traversed the rough roads, avoiding the inner areas of the city and taking the Ring Road that runs on the periphery. Onlookers would not have known or imagined it, but the truck contained the body of a king. In another break with norms, the body of Dipendra was being quietly taken to the royal cremation area where, two days ago, his entire family had been cremated with full honours. Today, the streets were deserted. His admirers would take it as the worst possible humiliation of Dipendra.

Prime Minister Koirala had faced much of the initial anger of the people, although it now seemed deflecting to King Gyanendra. The prime minister went on national radio. Unidentified 'anarchists' were trying to destabilize the country by spreading rumours, he said, urging peace.

Members of the Privy Council had now been summoned by the king for advice on a sensitive issue: following tradition, King Gyanendra would now declare his wife the queen. But should he also declare his unpopular son the crown prince? The members' counsel was clear: Don't.

The king was soon to hear of another casualty. His younger brother, Dhirendra Shah, who had struggled for life for three days, was pronounced dead at 5:57 p.m. at the Military Hospital.

At 9 p.m., state-run TV began playing a message recorded earlier by the king. The constitutional hurdle that he had faced earlier over revealing the facts had been removed. It would not be blasphemous to let Dipendra be named the killer. He was no more king. Shortly after King Dipendra was cremated ignominiously on the banks of the Bagmati, King Gyanendra's address began.

'Beloved citizens, I am extremely saddened to tell you that His Majesty King Dipendra is no more with us. In his tenure as King, we as Prince Regent had addressed you earlier. In that address, we had referred to the tragic incident at the Royal Palace on Friday, 19 Jyestha 2058, but there were constitutional and legal difficulties in expressing what had actually transpired. Now that the situation has changed, we will make an investigation into the incident and urgently let the beloved citizens know the outcome. We are convinced that all Nepalese must be solemn and united in living through these tragic times.'

King Gyanendra named a three-member inquiry commission that would investigate what had happened at the palace on the night of June 1. According to Nepal's Constitution, the government had no right to investigate any event inside the palace. The palace was also under no compulsion to carry out a public inquiry. However, forced by the circumstances, King Gyanendra had opened the gates of the palace to an independent civilian inquiry for the first time in its history.

In keeping with his typical man-in-a-hurry image, the king gave the panel just three days to complete its report. He also named the members: Nepal's chief justice, Keshav Prasad Upadhyay, Parliament Speaker Taranath Ranabhat, and an opposition communist leader, Madhav Kumar Nepal.

In the remote mountains of midwestern Nepal, the time seemed just right for 'Prachanda', the Maoists' supreme commander. Just like in 1990, when he had gone underground, passions were running high against the monarchy once again. It was a rare moment in Nepalese history. 'Prachanda' realized this and did an about-turn in his strategy in the days after the massacre.

The first move was to capitalize on the grief. 'Prachanda' sent an unprecedented salute to King Birendra, whose monarchy he had set out to destroy when the movement was started in 1996. 'Prachanda' started releasing statements backing King Birendra, and opposing Gyanendra.

He would say later in an interview with this author:

'In our opinion, King Birendra considered, from a feudal nationalistic point of view, the Maoist movement a patriotic movement. It is further justified by his reluctance to use the army against the Maoist movement, and stress on granting amnesty to the Maoists and resolving the issue through talks. About one month before the murder he had sent a message of his will to meet us through his youngest brother Dhirendra Shah, who was also murdered with him. We had a direct meeting with Dhirendra Shah only. A plan to hold talks directly with the late King Birendra was being worked out but it could not materialize due to his murder.

'According to our study, King Birendra held a patriotic and anti-Indian expansionism stand and politically, he was comparatively a liberal feudal. Hence, sometimes we would think that when the Maoist movement would be continuously developed, he may be asked, at a point, to play the role of the then Cambodian Prince (Norodom) Sihanouk, in Nepal.'

Another salvo had been fired the same morning, when a signed article by Baburam Bhattarai, the second-in-command of 'Prachanda', was published in *Kantipur*, Nepal's largest selling daily. Bhattarai was a frequent contributor to the paper. His op-ed piece called the massacre a 'grave political conspiracy' that it claimed had been backed by 'feudal and foreign forces' including Indian and American intelligence agencies. Bhattarai also compared the killings to the 1846 Kot Massacre. He urged the army to rebel against the king.

For 'Prachanda', the forty-seven-year-old son of a poor farmer, Gyanendra's installation would seem a setback to his campaign. It was widely known that King Birendra was soft on the Maoists; but his brother was known as a tough-going administrator famous for his determination. King Birendra had stalled army action against the Maoists for years.

The Maoist leader's article had created ripples among Kathmandu's intellectuals. The government now made another wrong move. In the evening, plainclothes policemen walked into the office of Yubaraj Ghimire, the paper's popular editor, and arrested him and two of the newspaper's top executives. These were the first such arrests in Nepal's decade of democracy and the free press.

Suspected Maoist activists continued to troop into the valley in crammed buses and trucks, but the situation seemed hobbling back from 'out-of-control' to 'manageable'. Several Maoist activists arrested by the police told their interrogators that thousands of their comrades were ready to sneak into the valley in the guise of mourners, driving in the night. A series of night curfews was imposed.

The inquiry committee had run into bureaucratic wrangles. Madhav Kumar Nepal submitted his resignation, saying he had not been authorized by his party.

The king was very upset. He accepted the resignation and asked the other two members to go ahead with the investigation. King Gyanendra also laid down the terms of reference of the committee, giving it a free hand to interrogate all witnesses, doctors and security officials, inspect the site and examine the weapons, spent bullets and all other confidential reports.

But another man had already decided to give his verdict.

On the afternoon of 7 June, journalists started getting calls in their hotels from unknown persons who asked them to reach the Military Hospital. They were promised interviews with the survivors. By 2 p.m., dozens of reporters and television crews had assembled outside the Military Hospital, waiting for the scoop. They were ushered in some time later, and asked to wait in a hall where a board had already been placed, with a sketch of the Billiard Room in black. Capt. Rajiv Raj Shahi, the army doctor and royal family relative who was also at the Friday night dinner, emerged some time later from the trauma hall in a T-shirt, his head shaven, a frown on his face.

Shahi was the first eyewitness who was going public with his account. He narrated the incident, blamed Dipendra for the killings, refused to take any questions, and then retreated into the hall. By the evening, he was facing a court of inquiry for speaking without authorization. But once he had spoken, other witnesses also started speaking out.

For eight days, the Billiard Room remained untouched. On the morning of 8 June, it received its first visitors after the massacre night. Accompanied by a video cameraman, still photographers and top officials and experts, the two members of the inquiry committee walked into the Tribhuvan Sadan.

It seemed they had walked into a mini-battleground. The shrieks of falling victims still seemed trapped within the high walls.

They walked in through the door, horrified at the remains of the carnage. As they looked across the room, it seemed a maniac gardener had sprinkled the entire hall with blood: there were blotches on the sofas, on the carpet, on the chairs, on scattered shoes and slippers, on crumpled coats and broken spectacles. Hundreds of cartridges were strewn across the room, on the carpet, beneath the chairs, and on the table. Bullets had riddled the walls, some punching through the framed paintings. There were glasses half full of whisky. There were loose earrings and hair clips.

At the site where Dipendra fell with a thud, the concrete carvings around the pond had been shattered. Water rippled over a pistol at the bottom of the transparent pond.

For the next several days, the committee members had unrestricted access to the palace. They interviewed the survivors, sat with ballistic experts and doctors, leafed through mounds of reports and official communication. They wanted to banish the ghosts of the massacre—the swirling conspiracy theories.

The priests were trying to do that, in their own way, on the banks of the Bagmati on the morning of 11 June—the eleventh day after King Birendra's death, when a dead person is believed to acquire the form of a spirit. The elaborate and rare 'katto' ceremony, held only for kings, would cleanse the monarch's soul on his way to heaven.

A seventy-five-year-old Brahmin priest, a vegetarian

all his life, would eat meat and become 'impure' today, and then be banished from the Kathmandu Valley, taking with him any vices of the king. The priest would never be able to perform religious ceremonies and would give up his profession. Beneath a large tent, the frail pundit, Durga Prasad Sapkota, took almost an hour to cook an elaborate meal for himself made of eighty-four ingredients. The meal is traditionally supposed to contain a part of the king's body too, but it is not known whether the practice was followed by Sapkota. He took barely nine minutes to finish his meal, and then started changing into his new clothes. He wore glittering clothes to resemble the king, an imitation of the crown, and several of King Birendra's actual belongings, including his shoes and spectacles. The priest was presented dozens of items to make his banishment comfortable: a sofa set, a cupboard, various sets of clothes, a bed, a table, and a transistor radio.

Then Prime Minister Girija Prasad Koirala walked into the tent where Sapkota was seated. He was following a tradition according to which the priest performing the ceremony is offered everything he desires.

'How are you? Do you have everything you need?' he asked. Sapkota had the answer ready.

'I am fine. I just don't have a house. Can I have a house?' he said. Sapkota would complain weeks later that he had not been given a house.

Sapkota then walked out of the tent, to a waiting elephant named 'Nirajan' after the dead prince. He struggled but finally managed to climb the caparisoned elephant, wearing the fake regal finery and King Birendra's dark glasses, as the elephant lumbered towards the river and waded across. The elephant, too, would now be his. Dozens of screaming children were assembled on the other side. They shouted and ran behind the elephant as it walked away.

Three days later, a similar ceremony was held for King Dipendra, but to the conservative priests, this one had seemed jinxed from the beginning. The elephant that was to carry this second Brahmin, Devi Prasad Acharya, had lumbered a long distance from the forests of Chitwan. On the way, on 10 June, a woman ran between its legs on a forest path—confident about the local superstition that this would help her conceive a child. The unsuspecting elephant was probably not aware of the belief; it got startled. As if uprooting stems of juicy sugar cane, the elephant scooped up the woman with its trunk and mercilessly threw her on the ground. She died instantly.

On the day of Dipendra's 'katto' ceremony, the vegetarian Acharya seemed indignant as he finished the meal, placed next to a goat's leg jutting out from a clay pitcher. As he clambered atop the elephant and started the journey towards the river, the elephant did something very unexpected: it trumpeted, turned around, and started walking up the gradient again, back to where it had come from. The mahout struggled and huffed, pulling the elephant's ear and goading it with his stick, and his antics seemed to have worked when the elphant turned around—briefly. Then it changed its mind again and swung back, the priest barely managing to cling on. The elephant was finally persuaded by the mahout to cross the river.

By the next evening, the inquiry committee members had done their bit of ghost-banishing too.

Upadhaya and Ranabhat, the two committee

members, walked briskly into the office of King Gyanendra. Due to the resignation of one member and the enormity of the investigation, the report had been delayed by more than a week from its original schedule. Upadhaya held a huge bundle of papers in his hands.

Soon, the two officials were at a crowded press conference where the five weapons found after the massacre were displayed on a large table. A steel box contained fat bunches of paper. The judge and the Speaker humoured the photographers by smiling and brandishing the weapons. They had not reached any conclusion in their inquiry. But the people they interviewed had no doubt that Dipendra was the murderer.

Upadhaya ended the press conference and packed. Nepal's estabishment had closed the chapter on the royal killings; they had declared Dipendra the assassin. But the people would take much longer—probably forever—to reconcile to the truth.

It was exactly what one could have expected from the no-nonsense administrator who became king. One of the first decisions that King Gyanendra took after assuming power was to scrap the 10 to 6 working hours at the Narayanhiti Palace, and ask his staff to follow a 9 to 5 timing. The offices were in the process of being redecorated. New furniture was ordered. Air-conditioners were being installed in the sultry rooms of the palace secretariats.

The monarch was in a hurry.

But time did not seem on the side of the new king when he took over on 4 June. The business leader and highly respected environmentalist had virtually been pushed into the role of king. He had the difficult task ahead of rebuilding trust in himself and his monarchy.

For a businessman and master troubleshooter, it was the most challenging assignment of his life. He had to take over the mantle of Nepal's most popular monarch ever. His job was made worse by the odds that were stacked up against him personally.

It did not help that King Gyanendra was the only Shah dynasty monarch to be enthroned twice. This time, King Gyanendra and his nation had started on the wrong foot with each other. Part of the reason was that he had kept a low profile over the decades, keeping himself restricted to his interests, and not much was known about him. It had become easy to feed stories into the vacuum of information.

Various people called him by various names. Fact and fiction were hard to distinguish in the fierce rhetoric that followed Gyanendra's succession. From taxi drivers to talkative housewives, ordinary people seemed certain that he was involved in some way in the palace massacre, that he had conspired for years to win back the throne he had lost in 1950. His communist opponents said he was an anti-democrat, a hardliner, who had tried his best to stop his liberal elder brother from giving democracy to the country. The media said he was a shrewd businessman who had had a controversial past. Pro-Maoists said Gyanendra had been linked in rumours decades ago to kickbacks given by businessmen to set up new businesses in Nepal. There were other allegations, some dating back to the Panchayat regime, in the effort to discredit him.

The new king was fighting several armies at the same time.

Gyanendra, fifty-four, is the middle son of King Mahendra. He was born on 7 July 1947, one and a half years after King Birendra, and went to the same school as his brother—St Joseph's College in Darjeeling. He graduated from the Tribhuvan University in Kathmandu in 1969, and then retreated backstage as his father groomed the elder brother to take control of the kingdom.

On 1 May 1970, three months after King Birendra married Queen Aiswarya, Prince Gyanendra got married to her younger sister, Princess Komal. The nineteen-year-old daughter of a revered army general had extremely simple tastes—housekeeping and flower decoration—and no inkling that she would be queen one day.

When King Mahendra died in 1972 and the crown prince succeeded him, Prince Gyanendra undertook his first major royal responsibility as the chairman of the committee that looked after the coronation. For the next three decades, the couple mostly kept away from the media glare, the prince travelling across the world on work, accompanied by his wife.

His first official visit abroad was in 1973, when he travelled to Germany for a conference on wildlife. Since then, he has spearheaded an international campaign for conservation. He is a leading light of the Worldwide Fund for Nature, formerly the World Wildlife Fund, and has addressed its meetings in different world capitals; he has addressed the Asia Society in New York; given a keynote address at the United Nations on the development of Lumbini, the birthplace of the Buddha; and has travelled to several countries on official visits or during royal funerals and weddings.

Back home too, he has had his hands full. King Gyanendra is probably Nepal's richest monarch ever.

Over the last three decades, he is said to have accumulated diverse business interests in several areas. The royal family has investments in some firms of the Soaltee Group, a business conglomerate that includes companies operating in sectors including tourism, tobacco, the tea industry, hydro-electricity, transport, market research and shipping. According to officials at the Soaltee Group, the royal family has stakes in the Soaltee Hotel, the Himalaya Goodricke Tea Company and Surya Tobacco. King Gyanendra is the chairman of the board of the tea company.

His critics demand that he give up his business stakes—something he would have to do in accordance with the Constitution—and disclose to the nation details about his corporate ventures. His close associates say his long experience as an administrator would help him in his new responsibilities as well.

In addition to his own earnings, King Gyanendra receives an annual remuneration of Rs. 10 million from the state, and inherited the properties of his elder brother. These include:

— The ancient Hanuman Dhoka Palace, Kathmandu
— The Patan Palace, Lalitpur
— The Gorkha Palace, Gorkha
— The 29-million-square-feet Nagarjun Hill, on which the Nagarjun Palace is also located
— The Ratna Mandir, or Temple of Jewels, at Pokhara
— Real estate in Kamaladi at the Kathmandu Plaza in the capital
— The Gokarna Safari Park
— Various plots of land and mansions.

Until 1990, even in the days of the monarchy's supreme power, Prince Gyanendra had few royal duties to perform. He temporarily held the chairmanship of the Regency Council during the absence of the king, and drove to the national day functions of several countries at their embassies, as he represented King Birendra. After the king gave up his absolute powers in 1990, Prince Gyanendra became much more private. He focussed entirely on his business interests, and what he loves most: nature conservation, reading and writing poetry, horse riding, a forest campfire, jungle tales and close friends.

His creative excellence is not surprising in a royal family in which almost each member has had achievements to show off. King Gyanendra is an eloquent speaker, especially in English, and he writes his own speeches.

His friends also say he is a quick and determined decision maker, who listens carefully to the other person's point, argues aggressively if he has different views, and then takes a decision. Most of his associates call him a 'dominating personality'.

Diplomats and officials who have held cocktail discussions and business dealings with him say Gyanendra is extremely well read, has the uncanny ability to select the right people for any job, and maintains a huge, well-stocked library.

He is described as very officious, and a stickler for protocol and decorum. 'Nothing should be haphazard when he is around,' a close acquaintance says.

Gyanendra is described by his work colleagues as very punctual—he normally reaches a meeting venue five minutes before time. Even if it is a meeting between four people who are informal among themselves, Gyanendra does not allow any letup on decorum. The participants will meet in a boardroom, seated around a table—not sitting casually, cross-legged on sofas. Pencils, notepads, glasses of water, background papers—everything must be in its proper place before the participants arrive.

At his first meeting with political leaders after assuming his position, participants said they were impressed by the businesslike approach of the new king. A top communist leader who has been Gyanendra's sharp critic said she came away with the impression that he was not an opponent of multiparty democracy, as had been portrayed earlier.

Apart from his no-nonsense, often ruthless professional side, Gyanendra has also indulged in creative adventures in the past.

He has written poems for years under the pen name of G. Shah. Gyanendra's poems have been published, composed and sung by prominent Nepalese singers, and an album of his songs was released by the state-run Nepal Radio.

In 1982, King Birendra established the King Mahendra Trust for Nature Conservation. He asked Gyanendra to look after it as the chairman, and to control the wildlife parks and forest reserves.

One of first projects suggested by Gyanendra was aimed at helping people living in the periphery of national parks, whose access to the preserves had earlier provided them livelihood and was now blocked. Experts said it showed sensitivity and a keen understanding of the complex issue of biodiversity.

He started several other projects, and the results

were quickly apparent. He established corridors for animals in the dense forests of Chitwan. He started discussions with authorities in India and China for cross-border help in tackling many shared wildlife issues. His biggest trophies include the successes in the campaigns to protect the one-horned Asian rhinoceros and the Royal Bengal Tiger.

Gyanendra's associates say that he seems obsessed with introducing better management practices in whichever project he undertakes. He introduced a corporate culture in the trust, and an emphasis on reward based on merit. The same qualities are expected to come into play in his new job.

It should be an able challenge for a king who believes: 'Life, as it is, is short, but it is made even shorter by waste of time.'

Far away from the maelstorm in Nepal, a young woman lay sedated on her hospital bed in New Delhi. She had eaten almost nothing for days. She refused to talk to anyone. Concerned relatives quietly streamed into the room and left. Strips of medicine were kept by her side. They did little for the pain in her heart.

Devyani Rana, the woman whose agony everyone forgot, had become the worst victim of Nepal's royal massacre.

Appendix I

An Interview with 'Prachanda'

FOLLOWING ARE EXCERPTS from a rare interview with 'Prachanda', supreme commander of Nepal's Maoist guerrillas, by the author.

'Prachanda', whose name means 'Fierce' in Nepali, gave written replies to questions sent through sources to his remote mountainous hideout in Nepal's midwest.

'Prachanda', forty-seven, was born Pushpa Kumar Dahal, the eldest of the eight children of Muktiram Dahal, a poor farmer in southern Nepal. He says his father's humiliation by feudal lords and urban creditors planted 'the seeds of class hatred and a sense of revolt' in him. He swiftly rose up the rungs of politics, and by the time the pro-democracy movement of 1990 started, 'Prachanda' had become the leader of one of Nepal's numerous communist groups. In 1996, he started a violent underground movement and now heads thousands of guerrillas fighting security forces to transform the Hindu kingdom into a republic.

'Prachanda' is described by his party as an 'expert in resolving disputes of the family, neighbours and friends' in his childhood and has had a keen interest in dancing, singing, soccer, volleyball and athletics.

Q. What do you feel were King Birendra's views on the Maoist revolution? Did you ever meet him? What are your views about him?

A. In our opinion, King Birendra considered, from a feudal nationalistic point of view, the Maoist movement a patriotic movement. It is further justified by his reluctance to use the army against the Maoist movement, and stress on granting amnesty to the Maoists and resolving the issue through talks.

About one month before the murder he had sent a message of his will to meet us through his youngest brother Dhirendra Shah, who was also murdered with him. We had a direct meeting with Dhirendra Shah only. A plan to hold talks directly with the late King Birendra was being worked out but it could not materialize due to his murder.

According to our study, King Birendra held a patriotic and anti-Indian expansionism stand and politically, he was comparatively a liberal feudal. Hence, sometimes we would think that when the Maoist movement would be continuously developed, he may be asked, at a point, to play the role of the then Cambodian Prince (Norodom) Sihanouk in Nepal. We firmly believe that this soft and liberal attitude towards us and tilting more towards China than India led to the massacre of his whole family. It is a plot designed by internal and external extremist reactionaries. It has further justified his patriotic and political liberalness.

Q: What do you feel about the future of monarchy in Nepal?

A: There is no future at all of the monarchy in Nepal. In our opinion, after the royal palace massacre, the traditional monarchy founded on feudal nationalism has also ended physically, legally, morally and from all points of view. In such a situation, there can be no question about the scope of monarchy. Gyanendra, who has been made 'king' of Nepal after the serious conspiracy, virtually represents oppressor classes, not the traditional monarchy. In fact, monarchy has gone away forever from the hearts of the people.

Q. Organization-wise, how strong is your campaign now? How does it compare with the Nepalese security forces?

A. Technically, the old regime enjoys a superior position in terms of, mainly, war logistics including arms. But what is notable is that the old regime and its security forces have been completely isolated from the masses. Besides, signs of discontent, protest and revolt have begun to appear in the Royal Army. Meanwhile, the People's Army is superior in terms of direct experience of war, moral sense of sacrifice, mass base, and organizational numbers. In such a state, the People's Army may worry the reactionary and make them tired for some time and ultimately may overcome them easily. The main question at this juncture is a direct and indirect cooperation to the reactionary by the foreign forces. In case of external intervention, the war may prolong for some time but we are confident that the People's Army shall turn out victorious ultimately.

Q. What has India's role been in the Maoist campaign?

A. The attitude and role of Indian ruling classes towards us has been completely hostile. They have been openly helping the corrupt rulers of Nepal against the People's War. India has been so prejudicial against the Maoist movement in Nepal and it intervenes in Nepalese internal politics. Even if the People's State is founded under the leadership of the Maoists representing the poor people in Nepal, it will not eat up India! The relation between the two countries will still be established on the basis of equality and freedom. What it exhibits is the extremely reactionary and expansionist behaviour of the ruling classes of India who boast of being the 'largest democratic' country. We demand that India stop interventions in the internal matters and make efforts to hold talks with us, the Maoists who actually represent the people of Nepal. If they stop helping the fascist and corrupt elements in Nepal, we are ready to hold talks even with the Indian government.

Q. You have called the new king Gyanendra the 'villain' in the palace massacre. Why?

A. Gyanendra has been called the villain of the heinous palace massacre not only by us, but by 25 million of Nepalese people also . . . As he succeeded in seizing the supreme body of the Royal Nepalese Army, some people due to fear and some due to some vested interests are not openly telling the truth.

Q. You have in the recent past suggested networking of South Asian groups fighting for independence.

A. The meeting of revolutionary parties of South Asia has been held. A coordination committee has also been formed as an organization at the South Asia level. In our opinion, this is a decision of far-reaching significance. Developing a united struggle against imperialism, mainly expansionist character of the Indian monopoly capitalism is an essential condition for the liberation and progress of all oppressed and exploited people in all countries of the region. Taking into account this historical need, we have been laying emphasis and advancing the democratic and national liberation movement in this region. Recently concluded meetings of the revolutionaries and their decisions are a very important first step in this region.

And Thus the Royals Fell

AS HE FACED his son's fury, King Birendra became part of a centuries-old juggernaut of royal tragedies that have shattered palaces across the world, most of them driven by clan enmity and the lust for power.

Many of these royal murders still wear shrouds of mystery and intrigue.

Until the 1920s, when his tomb was discovered in Egypt's mountains, historians knew little about the existence of the Pharaoh Tutankhamen, the boy king of the ancient civilization more than 3,000 years ago. Almost eight decades later, researchers are beginning to give voice to a secret long whispered in Egypt: Tutankhamen was murdered.

A 1998 book, *The Murder of Tutankhamen: A True Story*, by Bob Brier, cites historical evidence to recreate what it says was the assassination of the young king. Tutankhamen, eighteen, was sleeping in his bedchamber in a palace away from that of his queen, Ankesenamen. It was a breezy autumn night, and the only sound in the large, dimly-lit chamber, with sparse furniture and painted walls, was the drip-drip of the water clock. Deep into the night, unknown—or perhaps known—to the royal guards, a silent, stealthy shadow creaked open the door of the chamber. The king slept unaware, lying on his side, his head supported by an alabaster headrest. As the intruder stood by the boy king's bed, he took out a heavy object, possibly an Egyptian stone mace, that he brought down crashing on Tutankhamen's skull.

He did not die immediately. Royal surgeons examined the crack at the back of his skull, then gave up. The magic doctors and faith healers took over. Until the winter, Tutankhamen gained and lost consciousness, keeping his family and followers wavering between hope and despair. One day, he departed for heaven, and his body was embalmed and preserved for the coming centuries, and for his afterlife, in a tomb. The exact reason of his death, the manner of his killing—and the motive—will probably never be known.

Centuries later, one woman would be told the reason for her killing, but, as the hatchet came down on her, she would only have praise for the man who ordered it—the King of England. Anne Boleyn, one of the several wives of King Henry VIII, was publicly executed on 19 May 1536. She was thirty-six. Boleyn, whom the king secretely married in 1533, had attracted the attention of the king with her charm, sexual appeal and wit. Within three years, however, she was declared an adulteress and a witch, was dressed in a robe of black and taken to a public platform and beheaded.

Another prominent royal head was hacked in the next century, thousands of miles to the east in India. Mughal Emperor Shah Jahan had fallen seriously ill in 1658, provoking claims to the throne from all his sons—Dara Shikoh, 43, the crown prince, Shah Shuja, 41, Aurangzeb 39, and Murad, 33. In one of the worst succession battles in Indian history, Aurangzeb and his huge army clashed one by one with the troops loyal to his three brothers to decide who would rule over India. Aurangzeb defeated his elder brother Dara Shikoh and then took his own father prisoner, keeping Shah Jahan in a royal building in the city of Agra from where he could see the Taj Mahal. Aurangzeb defeated and killed the other two brothers soon. Dara Shikoh was soon captured by Aurangzeb. He was tried and convicted of sacrilege, and beheaded on the night of 30 August 1659. Within hours, Aurangzeb walked to the fortress where he had imprisoned his father, holding an unseemly gift: the severed head of Shah Jahan's eldest son.

In modern times, the killing of one royal sparked World War I.

Archduke Francis Ferdinand of Austria-Hungary was assassinated by a Serbian nationalist on 28 June 1914 as he travelled in a motorcade in Sarajevo, the capital of Bosnia-Herzegovina. Ferdinand was in the country to commemorate the 1389 battle of Kosovo—in which Turkey defeated and ended Serbia's independence. It was a humiliating anniversary for Serbians, who also were apprehensive that if Ferdinand succeeded to the throne, he would persecute the Serbs in his empire. Teenage terrorists from the underground group, the Black Hand, allegedly also linked to Serbian military intelligence, were lying in wait.

As Ferdinand's motorcade wound through Sarajevo roads, one Black Hand member tossed a bomb towards the archduke. Several things happened all at once. Ferdinand's alert chauffeur saw the explosive and pressed the pedal to avoid the impact. Sophie ducked. Ferdinand hit the bomb with his arm and deflected it. The explosive bounced off the car's rear and damaged the following car full of guards. The nineteen-year-old bomber—a boy identified as Nedjelko Cabrinovic—gulped cyanide and leaped into a river. However, he was detained before he could die.

The motorcade resumed its journey. The archduke had survived, but not for long.

Ten feet away, another Black Hand agent, Gavrilo Princip, stood ready. He stepped out and faced the car, lifted his pistol and fired two quick shots. He did not need more bullets. The first bullet hit Sophie, killing her immediately. The second greviously wounded Ferdinand, who died within minutes. Princip tried to kill himself but was captured too.

Austria's reaction to the assassination was quick and tough—it became an excuse for the government to crush Serbian nationalism. Germany's Emperor William II promised to back Austria in any such attempt. Within six weeks of Ferdinand's death, Austria-Hungary asked Serbia to fulfil a long list of difficult demands—in two days. The common thread that ran through these demands was: crush Serb nationalism. Three days after the deadline ran out and Serbia could not meet the demands, Austria-Hungary declared war on it. Russia backed the Serbs. France sided with Russia. Germany opposed France.

World War I began.

While the killing of one member of the royalty began the world war, its end paved the way for another royal assassination.

Before the clear Kathmandu night when Crown Prince Dipendra interrupted the Friday evening dinner with bursts of gunfire, one of the most gut-wrenching

royal massacres in history was the assassination of Czar
Nicholas II, Russia's last monarch, and six other members
of his family.

The 600-year rule of the czars in Russia ended in
humiliation on 14 March 1917 when Nicholas II, of the
Romanov dynasty, was forced to give up his throne.
Russia was steeped in poverty after being devastated in
the world war, and the czar was blamed for the
country's disgrace. A Duma, or Parliament, was in
place, and the country had a new administrator,
Alexander Kerensky. The czar was taken under house
arrest by guards who also detained his wife Queen
Alexandra, their daughters Olga, Tatiana, Maria and
Anastasia, and their only son Alexis. A Bolshevik
revolution, led by communist leader Vladimir Ilyich
Lenin, raged across the country, and the royal lives were
in danger. The czar and his family were swiftly moved
to Tobolsk in Siberia. In October 1917, Kerensky's
provisional government was toppled by the Bolsheviks.
By May 1918, the Romanov royal family had been
taken to a house in Ekaterinburg, a small town on the
slopes of the Urals.

Two months passed. On the night of 16 July 1918,
Russian officers ordered the royal physician, known
only as Dr Botkin, to move the family members to a
basement room, saying there was gunfire in the town
and riots were feared. The czar was woken up in the
early hours and asked to get ready. He did not suspect
anything. No one cried. No one asked questions. Guards
led the royal family and some of their servants—eleven
in all—to a chamber down the stairs. It was a large
room with no furniture. The queen was dismayed.

'What, no chairs? May we not sit?' she asked,

according to eyewitness accounts.

The commanding officer ordered two chairs, for the queen and her young son Alexis. The others were asked to stand in two lines—photographers were going to take their family photograph, they were told. Soon, several men described as photographers trooped in. They were eleven men, all Red Army sharpshooters. Each had been assigned a victim, whom they had to shoot through the heart to avoid excessive blood. However, they could not carry out the instructions.

They stood facing their victims.

An officer walked up to the deposed czar and read out his formal execution order: 'In view of the fact that your relatives are continuing their attack on Soviet Russia, the Ural Executive Committee has decided to execute you,' according to published accounts of eyewitnesses.

Nicholas, shocked and trembling, swiftly looked at his family, and then back at the officer.

'What? What?' he blurted. Those would become his last words.

Guards were posted in the neighborhood at posts some distance away. Minutes later in the darkness, the boom of seemingly endless rounds of gunshots echoed through the mountain town.

Like King Birendra, Czar Nicholas was the first to go down. The servant and two cooks were killed next. The Bolsheviks believed in shooting the messenger: Dr Botkin was also among those killed. Amazingly, the bullets bounced off the princesses. The firing squad did not know that the girls had sewn precious family jewels—in all, more than eighteen pounds of diamonds—into their corsets to carry around with them even in their custody. The terrified girls cowered and squatted on the floor, their backs pressed against the wall, their heads covered with their arms.

Two men fired at the girls' heads. Bullets also felled Alexis but he did not die immediately. The massacre was getting noisy and messy. The Bolsheviks did not want to arouse a whole town and convert the secret massacre into a public execution. Suddenly an officer rushed into the room and gave the next set of commands: bayonets.

The Bolsheviks stopped firing and aimed their bayonets at the survivors. In twenty minutes, it was over. The bodies were dumped in an old mine shaft, where the dead were all stripped, and the diamonds on the ladies' bodies collected. Soon after, the corpses were taken out from the shaft and buried in a mass grave in the town.

It was not the last carnage for the Romanovs. Bolsheviks executed seventeen other members of the royal family during the revolution. Blood had been spilled for centuries in killings in the Romanov dynasty: Czarevich Alexei, the eldest son of Peter the Great, was convicted by his father of treason and executed in 1718. Catherine the Great had her husband, Peter III, killed after she overthew him and occupied the throne. Ivan VI, twenty-four, who was briefly the monarch in 1741, was killed by his guards in prison in 1764. Paul I was suffocated by conspirators in 1801.

Meanwhile, mystery continued to surround the killing of Nicholas II.

In 1976, the grandson of one of the firing squad members guided officials to the mass burial site. The Communist Party ordered the city mayor to bulldoze the house in which the massacre was carried out. The mayor destroyed the house but suppressed information until 1991, when the Russian press first reported the story. The mayor was Boris Yeltsin, future president of the Rusian Federation. In 1998, the bodies were taken and buried again in St Petersburg in the cathedral where the other members of the family were buried.

Like King Birendra's death, the death of the czar and the Romanov royal family was also mired in superstition. There was also a dark prediction made by Grigory Rasputin, a Siberian monk who became the closest confidante of Queen Alexandra by miraculously curing prince Alexis' haemophilia—a blood disorder which prevents clotting and can make patients bleed to death if hurt.

Jealous relatives of the czar's family killed Rasputin on 31 December 1917, first by poisoning his food and wine and then shooting him repeatedly in the back. But days later, a letter was discovered from his home in which Rasputin had predicted his death—and warned that if he was killed, the czar and his family would also be killed within two years.

It took the Bolsheviks less than that to assassinate Nicholas II.

Decades away, 1975 was the year of two royal killings.

Saudi Arabia's King Faisal, a popular ruler, was attending a public meeting, called the *Al-Majliss* during which the ruler meets citizens every week. It was the morning of 25 March. As the king chatted with the people at the meeting, a man with a large frame loomed behind, walked up towards the king and brandished his .38 pistol. It was a nephew of the king, allegedly desperate to gain control of the kingdom's oil trade jackpot. He pumped three bullets into King Faisal at close range. As he fell, his body covered in blood, the king reportedly uttered his last words: 'I forgive you.'

Five months later, in August the same year, Ethiopian Emperor Haile Selassie I, eighty-three years old and king of forty-four years, died in mysterious circumstances, allegedly murdered by Marxist army officers who deposed him in a 1974 coup. The emperor was one of Africa's most charismatic leaders, believed to be the 225th monarch in a 2,000-year-old dynasty, a direct descendant of King Solomon and the Queen of Sheba.

In 1960, his son, Crown Prince Asfa Wossen, had led a failed coup against him. In 1974, there was another military revolt, which succeeded, and he had to step down. He died the next year. Like King Birendra, Selassie I was also considered god by his followers of the Rastafarian religion. To insult him, his assassins buried him near a lavatory—but he was reburied in 2000, twenty-five years after his death, in a solemn and colourful ceremony watched by thousands of people.

Four years later, more royal blood was spilled in Britain. It was the turn of Lord Louis Mountbatten, a member of the British royal family, who had served as the last British governor-general in India and presided over the historic and painful partition of the subcontinent that created Pakistan. He was also the great-grandson of Queen Victoria. Mountbatten's end came when he was cruising on a motorboat called *Shadow V* in a little harbour called Mullaghmore on 27 August 1979. It was a cheerful party, with three other peers, and the children. Mountbatten raced the boat, clearing the first of the lobster posts where they had aimed to reach. Then he slowed down.

There was a bomb ticking away, right beneath his feet. Fifty pounds of explosives, planted by the Irish Republican Army, were set to blow up the man who once controlled the destiny of millions.

Mountbatten was instantly killed in the explosion with two of the children.

The last of the major royal killings in the twentieth century took place on 25 April 1996, in Kwamashu, South Africa, in the ramshackle royal residence of Zulu King Goodwill Zwelithini. Armed attackers, believed to be led by a faith healer, stormed into the residence and bludgeoned nine members of the royal family moments after they had arrived from their country palace. The assailants were armed with traditional Zulu weapons, used for centuries in clan battles, such as sharp-edged machetes, spears and clubs called knobkerries.

The attack was gut-wrenching, even for a region that has seen years of grisly killings, massacres, clan and tribe attacks and counterattacks. Queen Buhle Mamathe Zulu, forty-five, the second of Zwelithini's five wives, was rammed on the head and she fell bleeding on the concrete porch in front of the house. Princess Sibusile Zulu, twenty-four, the queen's daughter, had her face slashed and a gunshot wound in her leg. The body of the king's cousin, Princess Nonhlanhla Zulu, thirty-five, was later found in a soccer field in the area. In all, seven royals were killed and the faith healer reportedly drank the blood of a dead princess.

Midway through the first year of the new millennium, the gunshots in the Narayanhiti Palace not only wiped out a royal family—they made a nation question its most abiding beliefs.

PENGUIN ONLINE

News, reviews and previews of forthcoming books

visit our author lounge

•

read about your favourite authors

•

investigate over 12000 titles

•

subscribe to our online newsletter

•

enter contests and quizzes and win prizes

•

email us with your comments and reviews

•

have fun at our children's corner

•

receive regular email updates

•

keep track of events and happenings

www.**penguinbooksindia**.com